HCG Diet
Tracker

This Book Belongs To

_____

Table of Contents

Sample of part of Daily Food Check list

Breakfast:	☐	Coffee	☐	Tea				

Lunch:

Protein (100 g):
☐	Chicken	☐	Veal	☐	Lean Beef	☐	Lobster
☐	White Fish	☐	Shrimp	☐	Crab		

Choice of Fruit:
☐	Apple	☐	Orange	☐	Strawberries	☐	1/2 Grapefruit
☐	Tomato						

Choice of Vegetable:
☐	Green Salad	☐	Cabbage	☐	Onion	☐	Chicory
☐	Fennel	☐	Cucumber	☐	Tomato	☐	Spinach
☐	Chard	☐	Celery	☐	Asparagus	☐	Red Radishes
☐	Beet Greens						

Sample of part of Meal / Calorie Logs

Dinner

_____   _____

_____   _____

_____   _____

_____   _____

_____   _____

Total Water Intake: _____   **Total Calories:** _____

Notes / Thoughts: _____

_____

_____

This tracker/ log book is not intended to be a how-to guide for the HCG diet. However, to make things easier for you, we have included some basic information on the HCG diet so you have it here for easy reference.

HCG Diet Overview

Phase 1 – Increase Fat/Calorie Consumption
Day 1-2
During the first phase of the HCG diet, you increase your caloric and fat intakes for two days, focusing on high-fat foods. At the same time, you will take HCG injections. The goal of the first phase is to interfere with the way the body stores fat. The HCG will prevent the fat from accumulating in your body, which begins the process of lipid mobilization.

Phase 2 – Radically Reduce Calories / Lose Weight
Day 3-26
On the third day of the HCG diet, you'll begin the second phase. At this point, you will drop your diet down to a 500-calorie regimen, eating only the foods outlined in the Simeons protocol. You will also continue with the HCG injection. The length of this phase depends on how much weight you have to lose. You should stick with the plan through twenty-three doses of HCG at a minimum. Your doctor will help you plan the doses. After you're finished with the HCG, you must remain on the 500-calorie diet for three days.

Phase 3 – Transition/Maintenance/Stability
Day 27-47
The transition phase is every bit as important as the weight loss phase. The purpose of the transition phase is to maintain metabolic function and customize your metabolic balance with your new weight. This phase lasts for three weeks and begins immediately after your last day of very low-calorie dieting. You will gradually increase your caloric intake to 1500 calories, making up 3 meals and snacks. It is important that these meals are comprised of healthy foods and spread out throughout the day. You may now consume any meats, eggs, fruits, cheeses, milk, vegetables and low sugar dairy products. Avoid foods with significant starches such as corn and potatoes. Avoid starches and sugar completely. When they

are combined, weight gain will occur drastically. It is important to note that your new weight has not yet become stable, meaning it will still show extreme fluctuations after an occasional excess eating.

During the transition phase, you may reintroduce healthy oils into your body such as flax seed oil, extra virgin olive oil and coconut oil. Avoid the unhealthy oils such as vegetable oil and shortening. Butter may also be consumed sparingly.

During and after the transition phase you should not gain any weight. If you gain more than 2 lbs from your LDW (Last Day Weight, the last day you gave yourself an HCG injection, do a Steak Day/ Correction Day.

Phase 4 – The Rest of Your Life
Life-time
This is the lifetime maintenance of the program. Continue to keep sugars to a minimum, introduce starches back to your diet very slowly and consume sugars, starches and healthy carbs in moderation. We recommend whole grains, oats, wheat bread, etc… Avoid heavy starch and sugars such as those found in potatoes, yams and rice.

Hydrogenated oils typically found in some canned goods and pastries should be avoided.

Strive to stay away from processed foods. Avoid high volumes of fructose syrup in such things as canned fruit, fruit drinks and soda. Continue to eat proteins and stay away from heavily processed or fast foods.

If you did not reach your weight loss goal during the 1st Cycle, you can now continue onto Cycle 2. This Cycle is a repeat of the 1st Cycle. The time off needed between each cycle will vary but is usually 2-4 weeks. After this break, you can continue until you reach your intended goal. Many individuals have lost in excess of 150 lbs over several courses of the diet.

\- HCG Diet Schedule -				
Day	HCG Injection	Food	Date	Weight
1	20 units	Unlimited		
2	20 units	Unlimited		
3	20 units	500 Cal Max		
4	20 units	500 Cal Max		
5	20 units	500 Cal Max		
6	20 units	500 Cal Max		
7	20 units	500 Cal Max		
8	20 units	500 Cal Max		
9	20 units	500 Cal Max		
10	20 units	500 Cal Max		
11	20 units	500 Cal Max		
12	20 units	500 Cal Max		
13	20 units	500 Cal Max		
14	20 units	500 Cal Max		
15	20 units	500 Cal Max		
16	20 units	500 Cal Max		
17	20 units	500 Cal Max		
18	20 units	500 Cal Max		
19	20 units	500 Cal Max		
20	20 units	500 Cal Max		
21	20 units	500 Cal Max		
22	20 units	500 Cal Max		
23	20 units	500 Cal Max		
24	Stop Injection Unless Advised	500 Cal Max		
25	None	500 Cal Max		
26	None	500 Cal Max		
27	None	No Starches or Sugar		
28	None	No Starches or Sugar		
29	None	No Starches or Sugar		
30	None	No Starches or Sugar		
31	None	No Starches or Sugar		
32	None	No Starches or Sugar		
33	None	No Starches or Sugar		
34	None	No Starches or Sugar		
35	None	No Starches or Sugar		
36	None	No Starches or Sugar		
37	None	No Starches or Sugar		
38	None	No Starches or Sugar		
39	None	No Starches or Sugar		
40	None	No Starches or Sugar		
41	None	No Starches or Sugar		
42	None	No Starches or Sugar		
43	None	No Starches or Sugar		
44	None	No Starches or Sugar		
45	None	No Starches or Sugar		
46	None	No Starches or Sugar		
47	None	No Starches or Sugar		

Day 1 : _____ / _____ / _____

20 Units of HCG and GORGE!

Morning Weight: _____

Directions: Eat as much fatty food as you can without making yourself sick. Enjoy your favorite fast food places, doughnuts, cake and candy! Be sure to include everything you think you may crave over the next month. Enjoy!

Notes/Thoughts:

_____

_____

_____

_____

_____

_____

_____

_____

_____

_____

_____

_____

_____

_____

_____

_____

_____

_____

Day 2 : _____ / _____ / _____

20 Units of HCG and GORGE!

Morning Weight: _____

Directions: Continue to enjoy being bad! Make a trip to your favorite restaurant and order all your favorite desserts. Even though you do not feel hungry due to the HCG being loaded into your system, it is still very important to keep eating to fill in your fat stockpiles. Just don't make yourself sick.

Enjoy today and be ready to change your life tomorrow!

Notes / Thoughts:

_____

_____

_____

_____

_____

_____

_____

_____

_____

_____

_____

_____

_____

_____

_____

Day 3 : _____ / _____ / _____

20 Units of HCG and 500 Calories

Morning Weight: _____

Breakfast: ☐ Coffee ☐ Tea

Lunch:
Protein (100 g): ☐ Chicken ☐ Veal ☐ Lean Beef ☐ Lobster
☐ White Fish ☐ Shrimp ☐ Crab

Choice of Fruit: ☐ Apple ☐ Orange ☐ Strawberries ☐ 1/2 Grapefruit
☐ Tomato

Choice of Vegetable: ☐ Green Salad ☐ Cabbage ☐ Onion ☐ Chicory
☐ Fennel ☐ Cucumber ☐ Tomato ☐ Spinach
☐ Chard ☐ Celery ☐ Asparagus ☐ Red Radishes
☐ Beet Greens

Starch: ☐ Melba Toast (Or 2 Melba rounds) ☐ Grissini Bread-stick

Dinner: Choose from the same menu as lunch but be sure and mix it up a bit--especiallyyour protein so you don't get tired of one certain food.

Protein (100 g): ☐ Chicken ☐ Veal ☐ Lean Beef ☐ Lobster
☐ White Fish ☐ Shrimp ☐ Chart

Choice of Fruit: ☐ Apple ☐ Orange ☐ Strawberries ☐ 1/2 Grapefruit

Choice of Vegetable: ☐ Green Salad ☐ Cabbage ☐ Onion ☐ Chicory
☐ Fennel ☐ Cucumber ☐ Tomato ☐ Spinach
☐ Chard ☐ Celery ☐ Asparagus ☐ Red Radishes
☐ Beet Greens

Starch: ☐ Melba Toast (Or 2 Melba rounds) ☐ Grissini Brestick

Misc: ☐ Tbsp Milk ☐ Juice of 1 Lemon ☐ Stevia Ultra Lean Comp. Shake 2
☐ Sugarfree Jello ☐ Mineral Water ☐ Club Soda With Stevia

YOU GOT THIS!

Breakfast   **Calories**

_____   _____

Lunch

_____   _____

_____   _____

_____   _____

_____   _____

Dinner

_____   _____

_____   _____

_____   _____

_____   _____

_____   _____

_____   _____

Total Water Intake: _____   **Total Calories:** _____

Notes / Thoughts: _____

_____

_____

_____

_____

_____

_____

_____

_____

_____

Day 4 : _____ / _____ / _____
20 Units of HCG and 500 Calories

Morning Weight: _____

Breakfast: ☐ Coffee ☐ Tea

Lunch:
Protein (100 g): ☐ Chicken ☐ Veal ☐ Lean Beef ☐ Lobster
☐ White Fish ☐ Shrimp ☐ Crab

Choice of Fruit: ☐ Apple ☐ Orange ☐ Strawberries ☐ 1/2 Grapefruit
☐ Tomato

Choice of Vegetable: ☐ Green Salad ☐ Cabbage ☐ Onion ☐ Chicory
☐ Fennel ☐ Cucumber ☐ Tomato ☐ Spinach
☐ Chard ☐ Celery ☐ Asparagus ☐ Red Radishes
☐ Beet Greens

Starch: ☐ Melba Toast (Or 2 Melba rounds) ☐ Grissini Bread-stick

Dinner: Choose from the same menu as lunch but be sure and mix it up a bit-- especiallyyour protein so you don't get tired of one certain food.

Protein (100 g): ☐ Chicken ☐ Veal ☐ Lean Beef ☐ Lobster
☐ White Fish ☐ Shrimp ☐ Chart

Choice of Fruit: ☐ Apple ☐ Orange ☐ Strawberries ☐ 1/2 Grapefruit

Choice of Vegetable: ☐ Green Salad ☐ Cabbage ☐ Onion ☐ Chicory
☐ Fennel ☐ Cucumber ☐ Tomato ☐ Spinach
☐ Chard ☐ Celery ☐ Asparagus ☐ Red Radishes
☐ Beet Greens

Starch: ☐ Melba Toast (Or 2 Melba rounds) ☐ Grissini Brestick

Misc: ☐ Tbsp Milk ☐ Juice of 1 Lemon ☐ Stevia Ultra Lean Comp. Shake 2
☐ Sugarfree Jello ☐ Mineral Water ☐ Club Soda With Stevia

YOU GOT THIS!

Breakfast   **Calories**

_____   _____

Lunch

_____   _____

_____   _____

_____   _____

_____   _____

Dinner

_____   _____

_____   _____

_____   _____

_____   _____

_____   _____

Total Water Intake: _____   **Total Calories:** _____

Notes / Thoughts: _____

_____

_____

_____

_____

_____

_____

_____

_____

_____

Day 5 : _____ / _____ / _____

20 Units of HCG and 500 Calories

Morning Weight: _____

Breakfast:	☐ Coffee	☐ Tea		

Lunch:

Protein (100 g):	☐ Chicken	☐ Veal	☐ Lean Beef	☐ Lobster
	☐ White Fish	☐ Shrimp	☐ Crab	

Choice of Fruit:	☐ Apple	☐ Orange	☐ Strawberries	☐ 1/2 Grapefruit
	☐ Tomato			

Choice of Vegetable:	☐ Green Salad	☐ Cabbage	☐ Onion	☐ Chicory
	☐ Fennel	☐ Cucumber	☐ Tomato	☐ Spinach
	☐ Chard	☐ Celery	☐ Asparagus	☐ Red Radishes
	☐ Beet Greens			

Starch:	☐ Melba Toast (Or 2 Melba rounds)	☐ Grissini Bread-stick

Dinner:

Choose from the same menu as lunch but be sure and mix it up a bit-- especiallyyour protein so you don't get tired of one certain food.

Protein (100 g):	☐ Chicken	☐ Veal	☐ Lean Beef	☐ Lobster
	☐ White Fish	☐ Shrimp	☐ Chart	

Choice of Fruit:	☐ Apple	☐ Orange	☐ Strawberries	☐ 1/2 Grapefruit

Choice of Vegetable:	☐ Green Salad	☐ Cabbage	☐ Onion	☐ Chicory
	☐ Fennel	☐ Cucumber	☐ Tomato	☐ Spinach
	☐ Chard	☐ Celery	☐ Asparagus	☐ Red Radishes
	☐ Beet Greens			

Starch:	☐ Melba Toast (Or 2 Melba rounds)	☐ Grissini Brestick

Misc:	☐ Tbsp Milk	☐ Juice of 1 Lemon	☐ Stevia Ultra Lean Comp. Shake 2
	☐ Sugarfree Jello	☐ Mineral Water	☐ Club Soda With Stevia

YOU GOT THIS!

Breakfast   **Calories**

_____   _____

Lunch

_____   _____

_____   _____

_____   _____

_____   _____

Dinner

_____   _____

_____   _____

_____   _____

_____   _____

_____   _____

Total Water Intake: _____   **Total Calories:** _____

Notes / Thoughts: _____

_____

_____

_____

_____

_____

_____

_____

_____

Day 6 : _____ / _____ / _____
20 Units of HCG and 500 Calories

Morning Weight: _____

Breakfast: ☐ Coffee   ☐ Tea

Lunch:
Protein (100 g):   ☐ Chicken   ☐ Veal   ☐ Lean Beef   ☐ Lobster
☐ White Fish   ☐ Shrimp   ☐ Crab

Choice of Fruit: ☐ Apple   ☐ Orange   ☐ Strawberries   ☐ 1/2 Grapefruit
☐ Tomato

Choice of Vegetable:
☐ Green Salad   ☐ Cabbage   ☐ Onion   ☐ Chicory
☐ Fennel   ☐ Cucumber   ☐ Tomato   ☐ Spinach
☐ Chard   ☐ Celery   ☐ Asparagus   ☐ Red Radishes
☐ Beet Greens

Starch: ☐ Melba Toast (Or 2 Melba rounds)   ☐ Grissini Bread-stick

Dinner: Choose from the same menu as lunch but be sure and mix it up a bit-- especiallyyour protein so you don't get tired of one certain food.

Protein (100 g):   ☐ Chicken   ☐ Veal   ☐ Lean Beef   ☐ Lobster
☐ White Fish   ☐ Shrimp   ☐ Chart

Choice of Fruit: ☐ Apple   ☐ Orange   ☐ Strawberries   ☐ 1/2 Grapefruit

Choice of Vegetable:
☐ Green Salad   ☐ Cabbage   ☐ Onion   ☐ Chicory
☐ Fennel   ☐ Cucumber   ☐ Tomato   ☐ Spinach
☐ Chard   ☐ Celery   ☐ Asparagus   ☐ Red Radishes
☐ Beet Greens

Starch: ☐ Melba Toast (Or 2 Melba rounds)   ☐ Grissini Brestick

Misc: ☐ Tbsp Milk   ☐ Juice of 1 Lemon   ☐ Stevia Ultra Lean Comp. Shake 2
☐ Sugarfree Jello   ☐ Mineral Water   ☐ Club Soda With Stevia

YOU GOT THIS!

Breakfast   **Calories**

_____   _____

Lunch

_____   _____

_____   _____

_____   _____

_____   _____

Dinner

_____   _____

_____   _____

_____   _____

_____   _____

_____   _____

_____   _____

Total Water Intake: _____   **Total Calories:** _____

Notes / Thoughts: _____

_____

_____

_____

_____

_____

_____

_____

_____

Day 7 : _____ / _____ / _____
20 Units of HCG and 500 Calories

Morning Weight: _____

Breakfast: ☐ Coffee ☐ Tea

Lunch:
Protein (100 g): ☐ Chicken ☐ Veal ☐ Lean Beef ☐ Lobster
☐ White Fish ☐ Shrimp ☐ Crab

Choice of Fruit: ☐ Apple ☐ Orange ☐ Strawberries ☐ 1/2 Grapefruit
☐ Tomato

Choice of Vegetable: ☐ Green Salad ☐ Cabbage ☐ Onion ☐ Chicory
☐ Fennel ☐ Cucumber ☐ Tomato ☐ Spinach
☐ Chard ☐ Celery ☐ Asparagus ☐ Red Radishes
☐ Beet Greens

Starch: ☐ Melba Toast (Or 2 Melba rounds) ☐ Grissini Bread-stick

Dinner: Choose from the same menu as lunch but be sure and mix it up a bit-- especiallyyour protein so you don't get tired of one certain food.

Protein (100 g): ☐ Chicken ☐ Veal ☐ Lean Beef ☐ Lobster
☐ White Fish ☐ Shrimp ☐ Chart

Choice of Fruit: ☐ Apple ☐ Orange ☐ Strawberries ☐ 1/2 Grapefruit

Choice of Vegetable: ☐ Green Salad ☐ Cabbage ☐ Onion ☐ Chicory
☐ Fennel ☐ Cucumber ☐ Tomato ☐ Spinach
☐ Chard ☐ Celery ☐ Asparagus ☐ Red Radishes
☐ Beet Greens

Starch: ☐ Melba Toast (Or 2 Melba rounds) ☐ Grissini Brestick

Misc: ☐ Tbsp Milk ☐ Juice of 1 Lemon ☐ Stevia Ultra Lean Comp. Shake 2
☐ Sugarfree Jello ☐ Mineral Water ☐ Club Soda With Stevia

YOU GOT THIS!

Breakfast   **Calories**

_____   _____

Lunch

_____   _____

_____   _____

_____   _____

_____   _____

Dinner

_____   _____

_____   _____

_____   _____

_____   _____

_____   _____

_____   _____

Total Water Intake: _____   **Total Calories:** _____

Notes / Thoughts: _____

_____

_____

_____

_____

_____

_____

_____

_____

Day 8 : _____ / _____ / _____
20 Units of HCG and 500 Calories

Morning Weight: _____

Breakfast:	☐ Coffee	☐ Tea		

Lunch:

Protein (100 g):	☐ Chicken	☐ Veal	☐ Lean Beef	☐ Lobster
	☐ White Fish	☐ Shrimp	☐ Crab	

Choice of Fruit:	☐ Apple	☐ Orange	☐ Strawberries	☐ 1/2 Grapefruit
	☐ Tomato			

Choice of Vegetable:	☐ Green Salad	☐ Cabbage	☐ Onion	☐ Chicory
	☐ Fennel	☐ Cucumber	☐ Tomato	☐ Spinach
	☐ Chard	☐ Celery	☐ Asparagus	☐ Red Radishes
	☐ Beet Greens			

Starch:	☐ Melba Toast (Or 2 Melba rounds)	☐ Grissini Bread-stick

Dinner: Choose from the same menu as lunch but be sure and mix it up a bit--especiallyyour protein so you don't get tired of one certain food.

Protein (100 g):	☐ Chicken	☐ Veal	☐ Lean Beef	☐ Lobster
	☐ White Fish	☐ Shrimp	☐ Chart	

Choice of Fruit:	☐ Apple	☐ Orange	☐ Strawberries	☐ 1/2 Grapefruit

Choice of Vegetable:	☐ Green Salad	☐ Cabbage	☐ Onion	☐ Chicory
	☐ Fennel	☐ Cucumber	☐ Tomato	☐ Spinach
	☐ Chard	☐ Celery	☐ Asparagus	☐ Red Radishes
	☐ Beet Greens			

Starch:	☐ Melba Toast (Or 2 Melba rounds)	☐ Grissini Brestick

Misc:	☐ Tbsp Milk	☐ Juice of 1 Lemon	☐ Stevia Ultra Lean Comp. Shake 2
	☐ Sugarfree Jello	☐ Mineral Water	☐ Club Soda With Stevia

YOU GOT THIS!

Breakfast   **Calories**

_____   _____

Lunch

_____   _____

_____   _____

_____   _____

_____   _____

Dinner

_____   _____

_____   _____

_____   _____

_____   _____

_____   _____

Total Water Intake: _____   **Total Calories:** _____

Notes / Thoughts: _____

_____

_____

_____

_____

_____

_____

_____

_____

Day 9 : _____ / _____ / _____

20 Units of HCG and 500 Calories

Morning Weight: _____

Breakfast: ☐ Coffee ☐ Tea

Lunch:
Protein (100 g):

☐	Chicken	☐	Veal	☐	Lean Beef	☐	Lobster
☐	White Fish	☐	Shrimp	☐	Crab		

Choice of Fruit:

☐	Apple	☐	Orange	☐	Strawberries	☐	1/2 Grapefruit
☐	Tomato						

Choice of Vegetable:

☐	Green Salad	☐	Cabbage	☐	Onion	☐	Chicory
☐	Fennel	☐	Cucumber	☐	Tomato	☐	Spinach
☐	Chard	☐	Celery	☐	Asparagus	☐	Red Radishes
☐	Beet Greens						

Starch: ☐ Melba Toast (Or 2 Melba rounds) ☐ Grissini Bread-stick

Dinner: Choose from the same menu as lunch but be sure and mix it up a bit--especiallyyour protein so you don't get tired of one certain food.

Protein (100 g):

☐	Chicken	☐	Veal	☐	Lean Beef	☐	Lobster
☐	White Fish	☐	Shrimp	☐	Chart		

Choice of Fruit:

☐	Apple	☐	Orange	☐	Strawberries	☐	1/2 Grapefruit

Choice of Vegetable:

☐	Green Salad	☐	Cabbage	☐	Onion	☐	Chicory
☐	Fennel	☐	Cucumber	☐	Tomato	☐	Spinach
☐	Chard	☐	Celery	☐	Asparagus	☐	Red Radishes
☐	Beet Greens						

Starch: ☐ Melba Toast (Or 2 Melba rounds) ☐ Grissini Brestick

Misc:

☐	Tbsp Milk	☐	Juice of 1 Lemon	☐	Stevia Ultra Lean Comp. Shake 2
☐	Sugarfree Jello	☐	Mineral Water	☐	Club Soda With Stevia

YOU GOT THIS!

Breakfast   **Calories**

_____   _____

Lunch

_____   _____

_____   _____

_____   _____

_____   _____

Dinner

_____   _____

_____   _____

_____   _____

_____   _____

_____   _____

Total Water Intake: _____   **Total Calories:** _____

Notes / Thoughts: _____

_____

_____

_____

_____

_____

_____

_____

_____

Day 10 : _____ / _____ / _____

20 Units of HCG and 500 Calories

Morning Weight: _____

Breakfast: ☐ Coffee ☐ Tea

Lunch:

Protein (100 g):	☐ Chicken	☐ Veal	☐ Lean Beef	☐ Lobster
	☐ White Fish	☐ Shrimp	☐ Crab	

Choice of Fruit:	☐ Apple	☐ Orange	☐ Strawberries	☐ 1/2 Grapefruit
	☐ Tomato			

Choice of Vegetable:	☐ Green Salad	☐ Cabbage	☐ Onion	☐ Chicory
	☐ Fennel	☐ Cucumber	☐ Tomato	☐ Spinach
	☐ Chard	☐ Celery	☐ Asparagus	☐ Red Radishes
	☐ Beet Greens			

Starch: ☐ Melba Toast (Or 2 Melba rounds) ☐ Grissini Bread-stick

Dinner: Choose from the same menu as lunch but be sure and mix it up a bit-- especiallyyour protein so you don't get tired of one certain food.

Protein (100 g):	☐ Chicken	☐ Veal	☐ Lean Beef	☐ Lobster
	☐ White Fish	☐ Shrimp	☐ Chart	

Choice of Fruit:	☐ Apple	☐ Orange	☐ Strawberries	☐ 1/2 Grapefruit

Choice of Vegetable:	☐ Green Salad	☐ Cabbage	☐ Onion	☐ Chicory
	☐ Fennel	☐ Cucumber	☐ Tomato	☐ Spinach
	☐ Chard	☐ Celery	☐ Asparagus	☐ Red Radishes
	☐ Beet Greens			

Starch: ☐ Melba Toast (Or 2 Melba rounds) ☐ Grissini Brestick

Misc:	☐ Tbsp Milk	☐ Juice of 1 Lemon	☐ Stevia Ultra Lean Comp. Shake 2
	☐ Sugarfree Jello	☐ Mineral Water	☐ Club Soda With Stevia

YOU GOT THIS!

Breakfast   **Calories**

_____   _____

Lunch

_____   _____

_____   _____

_____   _____

_____   _____

Dinner

_____   _____

_____   _____

_____   _____

_____   _____

_____   _____

Total Water Intake: _____   **Total Calories:** _____

Notes / Thoughts: _____

_____

_____

_____

_____

_____

_____

_____

_____

Day 11 : _____ / _____ / _____

20 Units of HCG and 500 Calories

Morning Weight: _____

Breakfast:	☐ Coffee	☐ Tea		

Lunch:

Protein (100 g):	☐ Chicken	☐ Veal	☐ Lean Beef	☐ Lobster
	☐ White Fish	☐ Shrimp	☐ Crab	

Choice of Fruit:	☐ Apple	☐ Orange	☐ Strawberries	☐ 1/2 Grapefruit
	☐ Tomato			

Choice of Vegetable:	☐ Green Salad	☐ Cabbage	☐ Onion	☐ Chicory
	☐ Fennel	☐ Cucumber	☐ Tomato	☐ Spinach
	☐ Chard	☐ Celery	☐ Asparagus	☐ Red Radishes
	☐ Beet Greens			

Starch:	☐ Melba Toast (Or 2 Melba rounds)	☐ Grissini Bread-stick

Dinner:

Choose from the same menu as lunch but be sure and mix it up a bit-- especiallyyour protein so you don't get tired of one certain food.

Protein (100 g):	☐ Chicken	☐ Veal	☐ Lean Beef	☐ Lobster
	☐ White Fish	☐ Shrimp	☐ Chart	

Choice of Fruit:	☐ Apple	☐ Orange	☐ Strawberries	☐ 1/2 Grapefruit

Choice of Vegetable:	☐ Green Salad	☐ Cabbage	☐ Onion	☐ Chicory
	☐ Fennel	☐ Cucumber	☐ Tomato	☐ Spinach
	☐ Chard	☐ Celery	☐ Asparagus	☐ Red Radishes
	☐ Beet Greens			

Starch:	☐ Melba Toast (Or 2 Melba rounds)	☐ Grissini Brestick

Misc:	☐ Tbsp Milk	☐ Juice of 1 Lemon	☐ Stevia Ultra Lean Comp. Shake 2
	☐ Sugarfree Jello	☐ Mineral Water	☐ Club Soda With Stevia

YOU GOT THIS!

Breakfast   **Calories**

_____   _____

Lunch

_____   _____

_____   _____

_____   _____

Dinner

_____   _____

_____   _____

_____   _____

_____   _____

_____   _____

Total Water Intake: _____   **Total Calories:** _____

Notes / Thoughts: _____

_____

_____

_____

_____

_____

_____

_____

_____

Day 12 : _____ / _____ / _____

20 Units of HCG and 500 Calories

Morning Weight: _____

Breakfast: ☐ Coffee ☐ Tea

Lunch:

Protein (100 g):	☐ Chicken	☐ Veal	☐ Lean Beef	☐ Lobster
	☐ White Fish	☐ Shrimp	☐ Crab	

Choice of Fruit:	☐ Apple	☐ Orange	☐ Strawberries	☐ 1/2 Grapefruit
	☐ Tomato			

Choice of Vegetable:	☐ Green Salad	☐ Cabbage	☐ Onion	☐ Chicory
	☐ Fennel	☐ Cucumber	☐ Tomato	☐ Spinach
	☐ Chard	☐ Celery	☐ Asparagus	☐ Red Radishes
	☐ Beet Greens			

Starch:	☐ Melba Toast (Or 2 Melba rounds)	☐ Grissini Bread-stick

Dinner: Choose from the same menu as lunch but be sure and mix it up a bit-- especiallyyour protein so you don't get tired of one certain food.

Protein (100 g):	☐ Chicken	☐ Veal	☐ Lean Beef	☐ Lobster
	☐ White Fish	☐ Shrimp	☐ Chart	

Choice of Fruit:	☐ Apple	☐ Orange	☐ Strawberries	☐ 1/2 Grapefruit

Choice of Vegetable:	☐ Green Salad	☐ Cabbage	☐ Onion	☐ Chicory
	☐ Fennel	☐ Cucumber	☐ Tomato	☐ Spinach
	☐ Chard	☐ Celery	☐ Asparagus	☐ Red Radishes
	☐ Beet Greens			

Starch:	☐ Melba Toast (Or 2 Melba rounds)	☐ Grissini Brestick

Misc:	☐ Tbsp Milk	☐ Juice of 1 Lemon	☐ Stevia Ultra Lean Comp. Shake 2
	☐ Sugarfree Jello	☐ Mineral Water	☐ Club Soda With Stevia

YOU GOT THIS!

Breakfast   **Calories**

_____   _____

Lunch

_____   _____

_____   _____

_____   _____

_____   _____

Dinner

_____   _____

_____   _____

_____   _____

_____   _____

_____   _____

_____   _____

Total Water Intake: _____   **Total Calories:** _____

Notes / Thoughts: _____

_____

_____

_____

_____

_____

_____

_____

_____

_____

Day 13 : _____ / _____ / _____
20 Units of HCG and 500 Calories

Morning Weight: _____

Breakfast: ☐ Coffee ☐ Tea

Lunch:
Protein (100 g): ☐ Chicken ☐ Veal ☐ Lean Beef ☐ Lobster
☐ White Fish ☐ Shrimp ☐ Crab

Choice of Fruit: ☐ Apple ☐ Orange ☐ Strawberries ☐ 1/2 Grapefruit
☐ Tomato

Choice of Vegetable: ☐ Green Salad ☐ Cabbage ☐ Onion ☐ Chicory
☐ Fennel ☐ Cucumber ☐ Tomato ☐ Spinach
☐ Chard ☐ Celery ☐ Asparagus ☐ Red Radishes
☐ Beet Greens

Starch: ☐ Melba Toast (Or 2 Melba rounds) ☐ Grissini Bread-stick

Dinner: Choose from the same menu as lunch but be sure and mix it up a bit--especiallyyour protein so you don't get tired of one certain food.

Protein (100 g): ☐ Chicken ☐ Veal ☐ Lean Beef ☐ Lobster
☐ White Fish ☐ Shrimp ☐ Chart

Choice of Fruit: ☐ Apple ☐ Orange ☐ Strawberries ☐ 1/2 Grapefruit

Choice of Vegetable: ☐ Green Salad ☐ Cabbage ☐ Onion ☐ Chicory
☐ Fennel ☐ Cucumber ☐ Tomato ☐ Spinach
☐ Chard ☐ Celery ☐ Asparagus ☐ Red Radishes
☐ Beet Greens

Starch: ☐ Melba Toast (Or 2 Melba rounds) ☐ Grissini Brestick

Misc: ☐ Tbsp Milk ☐ Juice of 1 Lemon ☐ Stevia Ultra Lean Comp. Shake 2
☐ Sugarfree Jello ☐ Mineral Water ☐ Club Soda With Stevia

YOU GOT THIS!

Breakfast   **Calories**

_____   _____

Lunch

_____   _____

_____   _____

_____   _____

_____   _____

Dinner

_____   _____

_____   _____

_____   _____

_____   _____

_____   _____

_____   _____

Total Water Intake: _____   **Total Calories:** _____

Notes / Thoughts: _____

_____

_____

_____

_____

_____

_____

_____

_____

Day 14 : _____ / _____ / _____

20 Units of HCG and 500 Calories

Morning Weight: _____

Breakfast: ☐ Coffee ☐ Tea

Lunch:

Protein (100 g): ☐ Chicken ☐ Veal ☐ Lean Beef ☐ Lobster
☐ White Fish ☐ Shrimp ☐ Crab

Choice of Fruit: ☐ Apple ☐ Orange ☐ Strawberries ☐ 1/2 Grapefruit
☐ Tomato

Choice of Vegetable: ☐ Green Salad ☐ Cabbage ☐ Onion ☐ Chicory
☐ Fennel ☐ Cucumber ☐ Tomato ☐ Spinach
☐ Chard ☐ Celery ☐ Asparagus ☐ Red Radishes
☐ Beet Greens

Starch: ☐ Melba Toast (Or 2 Melba rounds) ☐ Grissini Bread-stick

Dinner: Choose from the same menu as lunch but be sure and mix it up a bit-- especiallyyour protein so you don't get tired of one certain food.

Protein (100 g): ☐ Chicken ☐ Veal ☐ Lean Beef ☐ Lobster
☐ White Fish ☐ Shrimp ☐ Chart

Choice of Fruit: ☐ Apple ☐ Orange ☐ Strawberries ☐ 1/2 Grapefruit

Choice of Vegetable: ☐ Green Salad ☐ Cabbage ☐ Onion ☐ Chicory
☐ Fennel ☐ Cucumber ☐ Tomato ☐ Spinach
☐ Chard ☐ Celery ☐ Asparagus ☐ Red Radishes
☐ Beet Greens

Starch: ☐ Melba Toast (Or 2 Melba rounds) ☐ Grissini Brestick

Misc: ☐ Tbsp Milk ☐ Juice of 1 Lemon ☐ Stevia Ultra Lean Comp. Shake 2
☐ Sugarfree Jello ☐ Mineral Water ☐ Club Soda With Stevia

YOU GOT THIS!

Breakfast   **Calories**

_____   _____

Lunch

_____   _____

_____   _____

_____   _____

_____   _____

Dinner

_____   _____

_____   _____

_____   _____

_____   _____

_____   _____

Total Water Intake: _____   **Total Calories:** _____

Notes / Thoughts: _____

_____

_____

_____

_____

_____

_____

_____

_____

Day 15 : _____ / _____ / _____

20 Units of HCG and 500 Calories

Morning Weight: _____

Breakfast:	☐ Coffee	☐ Tea		

Lunch:

Protein (100 g):	☐ Chicken	☐ Veal	☐ Lean Beef	☐ Lobster
	☐ White Fish	☐ Shrimp	☐ Crab	

Choice of Fruit:	☐ Apple	☐ Orange	☐ Strawberries	☐ 1/2 Grapefruit
	☐ Tomato			

Choice of Vegetable:	☐ Green Salad	☐ Cabbage	☐ Onion	☐ Chicory
	☐ Fennel	☐ Cucumber	☐ Tomato	☐ Spinach
	☐ Chard	☐ Celery	☐ Asparagus	☐ Red Radishes
	☐ Beet Greens			

Starch:	☐ Melba Toast (Or 2 Melba rounds)	☐ Grissini Bread-stick

Dinner: Choose from the same menu as lunch but be sure and mix it up a bit-- especiallyyour protein so you don't get tired of one certain food.

Protein (100 g):	☐ Chicken	☐ Veal	☐ Lean Beef	☐ Lobster
	☐ White Fish	☐ Shrimp	☐ Chart	

Choice of Fruit:	☐ Apple	☐ Orange	☐ Strawberries	☐ 1/2 Grapefruit

Choice of Vegetable:	☐ Green Salad	☐ Cabbage	☐ Onion	☐ Chicory
	☐ Fennel	☐ Cucumber	☐ Tomato	☐ Spinach
	☐ Chard	☐ Celery	☐ Asparagus	☐ Red Radishes
	☐ Beet Greens			

Starch:	☐ Melba Toast (Or 2 Melba rounds)	☐ Grissini Brestick

Misc:	☐ Tbsp Milk	☐ Juice of 1 Lemon	☐ Stevia Ultra Lean Comp. Shake 2
	☐ Sugarfree Jello	☐ Mineral Water	☐ Club Soda With Stevia

YOU GOT THIS!

Breakfast   **Calories**

_____   _____

Lunch

_____   _____

_____   _____

_____   _____

_____   _____

Dinner

_____   _____

_____   _____

_____   _____

_____   _____

_____   _____

_____   _____

Total Water Intake: _____   **Total Calories:** _____

Notes / Thoughts: _____

_____

_____

_____

_____

_____

_____

_____

_____

_____

Day 16 : _____ / _____ / _____

20 Units of HCG and 500 Calories

Morning Weight: _____

Breakfast: ☐ Coffee ☐ Tea

Lunch:

Protein (100 g):								
☐ Chicken	☐ Veal	☐ Lean Beef	☐ Lobster
☐ White Fish	☐ Shrimp	☐ Crab	

Choice of Fruit:				
☐ Apple	☐ Orange	☐ Strawberries	☐ 1/2 Grapefruit
☐ Tomato			

Choice of Vegetable:			
☐ Green Salad	☐ Cabbage	☐ Onion	☐ Chicory
☐ Fennel	☐ Cucumber	☐ Tomato	☐ Spinach
☐ Chard	☐ Celery	☐ Asparagus	☐ Red Radishes
☐ Beet Greens			

Starch: ☐ Melba Toast (Or 2 Melba rounds) ☐ Grissini Bread-stick

Dinner: Choose from the same menu as lunch but be sure and mix it up a bit-- especiallyyour protein so you don't get tired of one certain food.

Protein (100 g):			
☐ Chicken	☐ Veal	☐ Lean Beef	☐ Lobster
☐ White Fish	☐ Shrimp	☐ Chart	

Choice of Fruit:			
☐ Apple	☐ Orange	☐ Strawberries	☐ 1/2 Grapefruit

Choice of Vegetable:			
☐ Green Salad	☐ Cabbage	☐ Onion	☐ Chicory
☐ Fennel	☐ Cucumber	☐ Tomato	☐ Spinach
☐ Chard	☐ Celery	☐ Asparagus	☐ Red Radishes
☐ Beet Greens			

Starch: ☐ Melba Toast (Or 2 Melba rounds) ☐ Grissini Brestick

Misc:			
☐ Tbsp Milk	☐ Juice of 1 Lemon	☐ Stevia Ultra Lean Comp. Shake 2
☐ Sugarfree Jello	☐ Mineral Water	☐ Club Soda With Stevia

YOU GOT THIS!

Breakfast   **Calories**

_____   _____

Lunch

_____   _____

_____   _____

_____   _____

_____   _____

Dinner

_____   _____

_____   _____

_____   _____

_____   _____

_____   _____

_____   _____

Total Water Intake: _____   **Total Calories:** _____

Notes / Thoughts: _____

_____

_____

_____

_____

_____

_____

_____

_____

_____

Day 17 : _____ / _____ / _____
20 Units of HCG and 500 Calories

Morning Weight: _____

Breakfast: ☐ Coffee ☐ Tea

Lunch:
Protein (100 g): ☐ Chicken ☐ Veal ☐ Lean Beef ☐ Lobster
☐ White Fish ☐ Shrimp ☐ Crab

Choice of Fruit: ☐ Apple ☐ Orange ☐ Strawberries ☐ 1/2 Grapefruit
☐ Tomato

Choice of Vegetable: ☐ Green Salad ☐ Cabbage ☐ Onion ☐ Chicory
☐ Fennel ☐ Cucumber ☐ Tomato ☐ Spinach
☐ Chard ☐ Celery ☐ Asparagus ☐ Red Radishes
☐ Beet Greens

Starch: ☐ Melba Toast (Or 2 Melba rounds) ☐ Grissini Bread-stick

Dinner: Choose from the same menu as lunch but be sure and mix it up a bit--especiallyyour protein so you don't get tired of one certain food.

Protein (100 g): ☐ Chicken ☐ Veal ☐ Lean Beef ☐ Lobster
☐ White Fish ☐ Shrimp ☐ Chart

Choice of Fruit: ☐ Apple ☐ Orange ☐ Strawberries ☐ 1/2 Grapefruit

Choice of Vegetable: ☐ Green Salad ☐ Cabbage ☐ Onion ☐ Chicory
☐ Fennel ☐ Cucumber ☐ Tomato ☐ Spinach
☐ Chard ☐ Celery ☐ Asparagus ☐ Red Radishes
☐ Beet Greens

Starch: ☐ Melba Toast (Or 2 Melba rounds) ☐ Grissini Brestick

Misc: ☐ Tbsp Milk ☐ Juice of 1 Lemon ☐ Stevia Ultra Lean Comp. Shake 2
☐ Sugarfree Jello ☐ Mineral Water ☐ Club Soda With Stevia

YOU GOT THIS!

Breakfast   **Calories**

_____   _____

Lunch

_____   _____

_____   _____

_____   _____

_____   _____

Dinner

_____   _____

_____   _____

_____   _____

_____   _____

_____   _____

_____   _____

Total Water Intake: _____   **Total Calories:** _____

Notes / Thoughts: _____

_____

_____

_____

_____

_____

_____

_____

_____

Day 18 : _____ / _____ / _____

20 Units of HCG and 500 Calories

Morning Weight: _____

Breakfast: ☐ Coffee ☐ Tea

Lunch:
Protein (100 g): ☐ Chicken ☐ Veal ☐ Lean Beef ☐ Lobster
☐ White Fish ☐ Shrimp ☐ Crab

Choice of Fruit: ☐ Apple ☐ Orange ☐ Strawberries ☐ 1/2 Grapefruit
☐ Tomato

Choice of Vegetable: ☐ Green Salad ☐ Cabbage ☐ Onion ☐ Chicory
☐ Fennel ☐ Cucumber ☐ Tomato ☐ Spinach
☐ Chard ☐ Celery ☐ Asparagus ☐ Red Radishes
☐ Beet Greens

Starch: ☐ Melba Toast (Or 2 Melba rounds) ☐ Grissini Bread-stick

Dinner: Choose from the same menu as lunch but be sure and mix it up a bit-- especiallyyour protein so you don't get tired of one certain food.

Protein (100 g): ☐ Chicken ☐ Veal ☐ Lean Beef ☐ Lobster
☐ White Fish ☐ Shrimp ☐ Chart

Choice of Fruit: ☐ Apple ☐ Orange ☐ Strawberries ☐ 1/2 Grapefruit

Choice of Vegetable: ☐ Green Salad ☐ Cabbage ☐ Onion ☐ Chicory
☐ Fennel ☐ Cucumber ☐ Tomato ☐ Spinach
☐ Chard ☐ Celery ☐ Asparagus ☐ Red Radishes
☐ Beet Greens

Starch: ☐ Melba Toast (Or 2 Melba rounds) ☐ Grissini Brestick

Misc: ☐ Tbsp Milk ☐ Juice of 1 Lemon ☐ Stevia Ultra Lean Comp. Shake 2
☐ Sugarfree Jello ☐ Mineral Water ☐ Club Soda With Stevia

YOU GOT THIS!

Breakfast   **Calories**

_____   _____

Lunch

_____   _____

_____   _____

_____   _____

_____   _____

Dinner

_____   _____

_____   _____

_____   _____

_____   _____

_____   _____

_____   _____

Total Water Intake: _____   **Total Calories:** _____

Notes / Thoughts: _____

_____

_____

_____

_____

_____

_____

_____

_____

Day 19 : _____ / _____ / _____

20 Units of HCG and 500 Calories

Morning Weight: _____

Breakfast:	☐	Coffee	☐	Tea			

Lunch:							
Protein (100 g):	☐	Chicken	☐	Veal	☐	Lean Beef	☐ Lobster
	☐	White Fish	☐	Shrimp	☐	Crab	

Choice of Fruit:	☐	Apple	☐	Orange	☐	Strawberries	☐ 1/2 Grapefruit
	☐	Tomato					

Choice of Vegetable:	☐	Green Salad	☐	Cabbage	☐	Onion	☐ Chicory
	☐	Fennel	☐	Cucumber	☐	Tomato	☐ Spinach
	☐	Chard	☐	Celery	☐	Asparagus	☐ Red Radishes
	☐	Beet Greens					

Starch:	☐	Melba Toast (Or 2 Melba rounds)	☐	Grissini Bread-stick

Dinner:

Choose from the same menu as lunch but be sure and mix it up a bit-- especiallyyour protein so you don't get tired of one certain food.

Protein (100 g):	☐	Chicken	☐	Veal	☐	Lean Beef	☐ Lobster
	☐	White Fish	☐	Shrimp	☐	Chart	

Choice of Fruit:	☐	Apple	☐	Orange	☐	Strawberries	☐ 1/2 Grapefruit

Choice of Vegetable:	☐	Green Salad	☐	Cabbage	☐	Onion	☐ Chicory
	☐	Fennel	☐	Cucumber	☐	Tomato	☐ Spinach
	☐	Chard	☐	Celery	☐	Asparagus	☐ Red Radishes
	☐	Beet Greens					

Starch:	☐	Melba Toast (Or 2 Melba rounds)	☐	Grissini Brestick

Misc:	☐	Tbsp Milk	☐	Juice of 1 Lemon	☐	Stevia Ultra Lean Comp. Shake 2
	☐	Sugarfree Jello	☐	Mineral Water	☐	Club Soda With Stevia

YOU GOT THIS!

Breakfast   **Calories**

_____   _____

Lunch

_____   _____

_____   _____

_____   _____

_____   _____

Dinner

_____   _____

_____   _____

_____   _____

_____   _____

_____   _____

Total Water Intake: _____   **Total Calories:** _____

Notes / Thoughts: _____

_____

_____

_____

_____

_____

_____

_____

Day 20 : _____ / _____ / _____
20 Units of HCG and 500 Calories

Morning Weight: _____

Breakfast: ☐ Coffee ☐ Tea

Lunch:

Protein (100 g):							
☐ Chicken	☐ Veal	☐ Lean Beef	☐ Lobster
☐ White Fish	☐ Shrimp	☐ Crab	

Choice of Fruit:							
☐ Apple	☐ Orange	☐ Strawberries	☐ 1/2 Grapefruit
☐ Tomato			

Choice of Vegetable:							
☐ Green Salad	☐ Cabbage	☐ Onion	☐ Chicory
☐ Fennel	☐ Cucumber	☐ Tomato	☐ Spinach
☐ Chard	☐ Celery	☐ Asparagus	☐ Red Radishes
☐ Beet Greens			

Starch: ☐ Melba Toast (Or 2 Melba rounds) ☐ Grissini Bread-stick

Dinner:

Choose from the same menu as lunch but be sure and mix it up a bit-- especiallyyour protein so you don't get tired of one certain food.

Protein (100 g):							
☐ Chicken	☐ Veal	☐ Lean Beef	☐ Lobster
☐ White Fish	☐ Shrimp	☐ Chart	

Choice of Fruit:							
☐ Apple	☐ Orange	☐ Strawberries	☐ 1/2 Grapefruit

Choice of Vegetable:							
☐ Green Salad	☐ Cabbage	☐ Onion	☐ Chicory
☐ Fennel	☐ Cucumber	☐ Tomato	☐ Spinach
☐ Chard	☐ Celery	☐ Asparagus	☐ Red Radishes
☐ Beet Greens			

Starch: ☐ Melba Toast (Or 2 Melba rounds) ☐ Grissini Brestick

Misc:			
☐ Tbsp Milk	☐ Juice of 1 Lemon	☐ Stevia Ultra Lean Comp. Shake 2
☐ Sugarfree Jello	☐ Mineral Water	☐ Club Soda With Stevia

YOU GOT THIS!

Breakfast   **Calories**

_____   _____

Lunch

_____   _____

_____   _____

_____   _____

_____   _____

Dinner

_____   _____

_____   _____

_____   _____

_____   _____

_____   _____

_____   _____

Total Water Intake: _____   **Total Calories:** _____

Notes / Thoughts: _____

_____

_____

_____

_____

_____

_____

_____

_____

Day 21 : _____ / _____ / _____

20 Units of HCG and 500 Calories

Morning Weight: _____

Breakfast: ☐ Coffee ☐ Tea

Lunch:
Protein (100 g): ☐ Chicken ☐ Veal ☐ Lean Beef ☐ Lobster
☐ White Fish ☐ Shrimp ☐ Crab

Choice of Fruit: ☐ Apple ☐ Orange ☐ Strawberries ☐ 1/2 Grapefruit
☐ Tomato

Choice of Vegetable: ☐ Green Salad ☐ Cabbage ☐ Onion ☐ Chicory
☐ Fennel ☐ Cucumber ☐ Tomato ☐ Spinach
☐ Chard ☐ Celery ☐ Asparagus ☐ Red Radishes
☐ Beet Greens

Starch: ☐ Melba Toast (Or 2 Melba rounds) ☐ Grissini Bread-stick

Dinner: Choose from the same menu as lunch but be sure and mix it up a bit-- especially your protein so you don't get tired of one certain food.

Protein (100 g): ☐ Chicken ☐ Veal ☐ Lean Beef ☐ Lobster
☐ White Fish ☐ Shrimp ☐ Chart

Choice of Fruit: ☐ Apple ☐ Orange ☐ Strawberries ☐ 1/2 Grapefruit

Choice of Vegetable: ☐ Green Salad ☐ Cabbage ☐ Onion ☐ Chicory
☐ Fennel ☐ Cucumber ☐ Tomato ☐ Spinach
☐ Chard ☐ Celery ☐ Asparagus ☐ Red Radishes
☐ Beet Greens

Starch: ☐ Melba Toast (Or 2 Melba rounds) ☐ Grissini Brestick

Misc: ☐ Tbsp Milk ☐ Juice of 1 Lemon ☐ Stevia Ultra Lean Comp. Shake 2
☐ Sugarfree Jello ☐ Mineral Water ☐ Club Soda With Stevia

YOU GOT THIS!

Breakfast   **Calories**

_____   _____

Lunch

_____   _____

_____   _____

_____   _____

_____   _____

Dinner

_____   _____

_____   _____

_____   _____

_____   _____

_____   _____

Total Water Intake: _____   **Total Calories:** _____

Notes / Thoughts: _____

_____

_____

_____

_____

_____

_____

_____

_____

Day 22 : _____ / _____ / _____

20 Units of HCG and 500 Calories

Morning Weight: _____

Breakfast: ☐ Coffee ☐ Tea

Lunch:
Protein (100 g): ☐ Chicken ☐ Veal ☐ Lean Beef ☐ Lobster
☐ White Fish ☐ Shrimp ☐ Crab

Choice of Fruit: ☐ Apple ☐ Orange ☐ Strawberries ☐ 1/2 Grapefruit
☐ Tomato

Choice of Vegetable: ☐ Green Salad ☐ Cabbage ☐ Onion ☐ Chicory
☐ Fennel ☐ Cucumber ☐ Tomato ☐ Spinach
☐ Chard ☐ Celery ☐ Asparagus ☐ Red Radishes
☐ Beet Greens

Starch: ☐ Melba Toast (Or 2 Melba rounds) ☐ Grissini Bread-stick

Dinner: Choose from the same menu as lunch but be sure and mix it up a bit-- especiallyyour protein so you don't get tired of one certain food.

Protein (100 g): ☐ Chicken ☐ Veal ☐ Lean Beef ☐ Lobster
☐ White Fish ☐ Shrimp ☐ Chart

Choice of Fruit: ☐ Apple ☐ Orange ☐ Strawberries ☐ 1/2 Grapefruit

Choice of Vegetable: ☐ Green Salad ☐ Cabbage ☐ Onion ☐ Chicory
☐ Fennel ☐ Cucumber ☐ Tomato ☐ Spinach
☐ Chard ☐ Celery ☐ Asparagus ☐ Red Radishes
☐ Beet Greens

Starch: ☐ Melba Toast (Or 2 Melba rounds) ☐ Grissini Brestick

Misc: ☐ Tbsp Milk ☐ Juice of 1 Lemon ☐ Stevia Ultra Lean Comp. Shake 2
☐ Sugarfree Jello ☐ Mineral Water ☐ Club Soda With Stevia

YOU GOT THIS!

Breakfast   **Calories**

_____   _____

Lunch

_____   _____

_____   _____

_____   _____

_____   _____

Dinner

_____   _____

_____   _____

_____   _____

_____   _____

_____   _____

_____   _____

Total Water Intake: _____   **Total Calories:** _____

Notes / Thoughts: _____

_____

_____

_____

_____

_____

_____

_____

_____

Day 23 : _____ / _____ / _____
20 Units of HCG and 500 Calories

Morning Weight: _____

Breakfast: ☐ Coffee ☐ Tea

Lunch:
Protein (100 g): ☐ Chicken ☐ Veal ☐ Lean Beef ☐ Lobster
☐ White Fish ☐ Shrimp ☐ Crab

Choice of Fruit: ☐ Apple ☐ Orange ☐ Strawberries ☐ 1/2 Grapefruit
☐ Tomato

Choice of Vegetable: ☐ Green Salad ☐ Cabbage ☐ Onion ☐ Chicory
☐ Fennel ☐ Cucumber ☐ Tomato ☐ Spinach
☐ Chard ☐ Celery ☐ Asparagus ☐ Red Radishes
☐ Beet Greens

Starch: ☐ Melba Toast (Or 2 Melba rounds) ☐ Grissini Bread-stick

Dinner: Choose from the same menu as lunch but be sure and mix it up a bit-- especiallyyour protein so you don't get tired of one certain food.

Protein (100 g): ☐ Chicken ☐ Veal ☐ Lean Beef ☐ Lobster
☐ White Fish ☐ Shrimp ☐ Chart

Choice of Fruit: ☐ Apple ☐ Orange ☐ Strawberries ☐ 1/2 Grapefruit

Choice of Vegetable: ☐ Green Salad ☐ Cabbage ☐ Onion ☐ Chicory
☐ Fennel ☐ Cucumber ☐ Tomato ☐ Spinach
☐ Chard ☐ Celery ☐ Asparagus ☐ Red Radishes
☐ Beet Greens

Starch: ☐ Melba Toast (Or 2 Melba rounds) ☐ Grissini Brestick

Misc: ☐ Tbsp Milk ☐ Juice of 1 Lemon ☐ Stevia Ultra Lean Comp. Shake 2
☐ Sugarfree Jello ☐ Mineral Water ☐ Club Soda With Stevia

YOU GOT THIS!

Breakfast   **Calories**

_____   _____

Lunch

_____   _____

_____   _____

_____   _____

_____   _____

Dinner

_____   _____

_____   _____

_____   _____

_____   _____

_____   _____

Total Water Intake: _____   **Total Calories:** _____

Notes / Thoughts: _____

_____

_____

_____

_____

_____

_____

_____

_____

Day 24 : _____ / _____ / _____
20 Units of HCG and 500 Calories

Morning Weight: _____

Breakfast: ☐ Coffee ☐ Tea

Lunch:

Protein (100 g):

☐ Chicken	☐ Veal	☐ Lean Beef	☐ Lobster
☐ White Fish	☐ Shrimp	☐ Crab	

Choice of Fruit:

☐ Apple	☐ Orange	☐ Strawberries	☐ 1/2 Grapefruit
☐ Tomato			

Choice of Vegetable:

☐ Green Salad	☐ Cabbage	☐ Onion	☐ Chicory
☐ Fennel	☐ Cucumber	☐ Tomato	☐ Spinach
☐ Chard	☐ Celery	☐ Asparagus	☐ Red Radishes
☐ Beet Greens			

Starch: ☐ Melba Toast (Or 2 Melba rounds) ☐ Grissini Bread-stick

Dinner: Choose from the same menu as lunch but be sure and mix it up a bit-- especiallyyour protein so you don't get tired of one certain food.

Protein (100 g):

☐ Chicken	☐ Veal	☐ Lean Beef	☐ Lobster
☐ White Fish	☐ Shrimp	☐ Chart	

Choice of Fruit:

☐ Apple	☐ Orange	☐ Strawberries	☐ 1/2 Grapefruit

Choice of Vegetable:

☐ Green Salad	☐ Cabbage	☐ Onion	☐ Chicory
☐ Fennel	☐ Cucumber	☐ Tomato	☐ Spinach
☐ Chard	☐ Celery	☐ Asparagus	☐ Red Radishes
☐ Beet Greens			

Starch: ☐ Melba Toast (Or 2 Melba rounds) ☐ Grissini Brestick

Misc:

☐ Tbsp Milk	☐ Juice of 1 Lemon	☐ Stevia Ultra Lean Comp. Shake 2
☐ Sugarfree Jello	☐ Mineral Water	☐ Club Soda With Stevia

YOU GOT THIS!

Breakfast   **Calories**

_____   _____

Lunch

_____   _____

_____   _____

_____   _____

_____   _____

Dinner

_____   _____

_____   _____

_____   _____

_____   _____

_____   _____

_____   _____

Total Water Intake: _____   **Total Calories:** _____

Notes / Thoughts: _____

_____

_____

_____

_____

_____

_____

_____

_____

Day 25 : _____ / _____ / _____

20 Units of HCG and 500 Calories

Morning Weight: _____

Breakfast:	☐ Coffee	☐ Tea		

Lunch:

Protein (100 g):	☐ Chicken	☐ Veal	☐ Lean Beef	☐ Lobster
	☐ White Fish	☐ Shrimp	☐ Crab	

Choice of Fruit:	☐ Apple	☐ Orange	☐ Strawberries	☐ 1/2 Grapefruit
	☐ Tomato			

Choice of Vegetable:	☐ Green Salad	☐ Cabbage	☐ Onion	☐ Chicory
	☐ Fennel	☐ Cucumber	☐ Tomato	☐ Spinach
	☐ Chard	☐ Celery	☐ Asparagus	☐ Red Radishes
	☐ Beet Greens			

Starch:	☐ Melba Toast (Or 2 Melba rounds)	☐ Grissini Bread-stick

Dinner: Choose from the same menu as lunch but be sure and mix it up a bit--especiallyyour protein so you don't get tired of one certain food.

Protein (100 g):	☐ Chicken	☐ Veal	☐ Lean Beef	☐ Lobster
	☐ White Fish	☐ Shrimp	☐ Chart	

Choice of Fruit:	☐ Apple	☐ Orange	☐ Strawberries	☐ 1/2 Grapefruit

Choice of Vegetable:	☐ Green Salad	☐ Cabbage	☐ Onion	☐ Chicory
	☐ Fennel	☐ Cucumber	☐ Tomato	☐ Spinach
	☐ Chard	☐ Celery	☐ Asparagus	☐ Red Radishes
	☐ Beet Greens			

Starch:	☐ Melba Toast (Or 2 Melba rounds)	☐ Grissini Brestick

Misc:	☐ Tbsp Milk	☐ Juice of 1 Lemon	☐ Stevia Ultra Lean Comp. Shake 2
	☐ Sugarfree Jello	☐ Mineral Water	☐ Club Soda With Stevia

YOU GOT THIS!

Breakfast   **Calories**

_____   _____

Lunch

_____   _____

_____   _____

_____   _____

_____   _____

Dinner

_____   _____

_____   _____

_____   _____

_____   _____

_____   _____

_____   _____

Total Water Intake: _____   **Total Calories:** _____

Notes / Thoughts: _____

_____

_____

_____

_____

_____

_____

_____

_____

_____

Day 26 : _____ / _____ / _____

20 Units of HCG and 500 Calories

Morning Weight: _____

Breakfast: ☐ Coffee   ☐ Tea

Lunch:

Protein (100 g):	☐ Chicken	☐ Veal	☐ Lean Beef	☐ Lobster
	☐ White Fish	☐ Shrimp	☐ Crab	

Choice of Fruit:	☐ Apple	☐ Orange	☐ Strawberries	☐ 1/2 Grapefruit
	☐ Tomato			

Choice of Vegetable:	☐ Green Salad	☐ Cabbage	☐ Onion	☐ Chicory
	☐ Fennel	☐ Cucumber	☐ Tomato	☐ Spinach
	☐ Chard	☐ Celery	☐ Asparagus	☐ Red Radishes
	☐ Beet Greens			

Starch: ☐ Melba Toast (Or 2 Melba rounds)   ☐ Grissini Bread-stick

Dinner: Choose from the same menu as lunch but be sure and mix it up a bit-- especiallyyour protein so you don't get tired of one certain food.

Protein (100 g):	☐ Chicken	☐ Veal	☐ Lean Beef	☐ Lobster
	☐ White Fish	☐ Shrimp	☐ Chart	

Choice of Fruit:	☐ Apple	☐ Orange	☐ Strawberries	☐ 1/2 Grapefruit

Choice of Vegetable:	☐ Green Salad	☐ Cabbage	☐ Onion	☐ Chicory
	☐ Fennel	☐ Cucumber	☐ Tomato	☐ Spinach
	☐ Chard	☐ Celery	☐ Asparagus	☐ Red Radishes
	☐ Beet Greens			

Starch: ☐ Melba Toast (Or 2 Melba rounds)   ☐ Grissini Brestick

Misc:	☐ Tbsp Milk	☐ Juice of 1 Lemon	☐ Stevia Ultra Lean Comp. Shake 2
	☐ Sugarfree Jello	☐ Mineral Water	☐ Club Soda With Stevia

YOU GOT THIS!

Breakfast   **Calories**

_____   _____

Lunch

_____   _____

_____   _____

_____   _____

_____   _____

Dinner

_____   _____

_____   _____

_____   _____

_____   _____

_____   _____

_____   _____

Total Water Intake: _____   **Total Calories:** _____

Notes / Thoughts: _____

_____

_____

_____

_____

_____

_____

_____

_____

Day 27 : _____ / _____ / _____

CONGRATULATIONS! YOU MADE IT!

Aim for 550 calories today

Morning Weight: _____

You are now in Phase 3 – Maintenance/Transition/Stability

This transition phase is every bit as important as the weight loss phase. The purpose of the transition phase is to maintain metabolic function and customize your metabolic balance with your new weight. This phase lasts for three weeks and begins now. You will gradually increase your caloric intake to 1500 calories from 3 meals and snacks. It is important that these meals are comprised of healthy foods and spread out throughout the day. You may now consume any meats, eggs, fruits, cheeses, milk, vegetables and low sugar dairy products. Avoid foods with significant starches such as corn and potatoes. Stay away from sugar completely. When starches and sugar are combined, weight gain will occur drastically. It is important to note that your new weight has not yet become stable. In other words, it will still show extreme fluctuations after an occasional excess eating.

During the transition phase, you may reintroduce healthy oils into your body such as flax seed oil, extra virgin olive oil and coconut oil. Avoid the unhealthy oils such as vegetable oil and shortening. Butter may also be consumed sparingly.

During and after the transition phase you should not gain any weight. If you gain more than 2 lbs from your LDW (Last Day Weight, the last day you gave yourself an HCG injection, do a Steak Day/ Correction Day.

Breakfast	Calories

Lunch

_____ _____

_____ _____

_____ _____

_____ _____

Dinner

_____ _____

_____ _____

_____ _____

_____ _____

_____ _____

Snacks

_____ _____

_____ _____

Total Water Intake: _____   **Total Calories:** _____

Notes / Thoughts: _____

_____

_____

_____

_____

_____

_____

Day 28 : _____ / _____ / _____

Keep Eating Healthy!
Aim for 600 calories

Morning Weight: _____

This transition phase is *every bit as important as the weight loss phase*. The purpose of the transition phase is to maintain metabolic function and customize your metabolic balance with your new weight.

Gradually increase your caloric intake to 1500 calories from 3 meals and snacks. It is important that these meals are comprised of healthy foods and spread out throughout the day. You may now consume any meats, eggs, fruits, cheeses, milk, vegetables and low sugar dairy products. Avoid foods with significant starches such as corn and potatoes. Stay away from sugar completely. When starches and sugar are combined, weight gain will occur drastically. It is important to note that your new weight has not yet become stable. In other words, it will still show extreme fluctuations after an occasional excess eating. Reintroduce healthy oils into your body such as flax seed oil, extra virgin olive oil and coconut oil. Avoid the unhealthy oils such as vegetable oil and shortening. Butter may also be consumed sparingly.

During and after the transition phase you should not gain any weight. If you gain more than 2 lbs from your LDW (Last Day Weight, the last day you gave yourself an HCG injection, do a Steak Day/ Correction Day.

Breakfast   **Calories**

_____   _____

_____   _____

_____   _____

_____   _____

Lunch

_____   _____

_____   _____

_____   _____

_____   _____

_____   _____

Dinner

_____   _____

_____   _____

_____   _____

_____   _____

_____   _____

_____   _____

Snacks

_____   _____

_____   _____

Total Water Intake: _____   **Total Calories:** _____

Notes / Thoughts: _____

_____

_____

_____

_____

_____

_____

_____

_____

_____

_____

Day 29 : _____ / _____ / _____

Keep Eating Healthy!

Aim for 650 calories

Morning Weight: _____

This transition phase is _every bit as important as the weight loss phase_. The purpose of the transition phase is to maintain metabolic function and customize your metabolic balance with your new weight.

Gradually increase your caloric intake to 1500 calories from 3 meals and snacks. It is important that these meals are comprised of healthy foods and spread out throughout the day. You may now consume any meats, eggs, fruits, cheeses, milk, vegetables and low sugar dairy products. Avoid foods with significant starches such as corn and potatoes. Stay away from sugar completely. When starches and sugar are combined, weight gain will occur drastically. It is important to note that your new weight has not yet become stable. In other words, it will still show extreme fluctuations after an occasional excess eating. Reintroduce healthy oils into your body such as flax seed oil, extra virgin olive oil and coconut oil. Avoid the unhealthy oils such as vegetable oil and shortening. Butter may also be consumed sparingly.

During and after the transition phase you should not gain any weight. If you gain more than 2 lbs from your LDW (Last Day Weight, the last day you gave yourself an HCG injection, do a Steak Day/ Correction Day.

Breakfast   **Calories**

_____   _____

_____   _____

_____   _____

_____   _____

Lunch

_____   _____

_____   _____

_____ _____

_____ _____

_____ _____

Dinner

_____ _____

_____ _____

_____ _____

_____ _____

_____ _____

Snacks

_____ _____

_____ _____

Total Water Intake: _____   **Total Calories:** _____

Notes / Thoughts: _____

_____

_____

_____

_____

_____

_____

_____

_____

_____

Day 30 : _____ / _____ / _____

Keep Eating Healthy!

Aim for 700 calories

Morning Weight: _____

This transition phase is *every bit as important as the weight loss phase*. The purpose of the transition phase is to maintain metabolic function and customize your metabolic balance with your new weight.

Gradually increase your caloric intake to 1500 calories from 3 meals and snacks. It is important that these meals are comprised of healthy foods and spread out throughout the day. You may now consume any meats, eggs, fruits, cheeses, milk, vegetables and low sugar dairy products. Avoid foods with significant starches such as corn and potatoes. Stay away from sugar completely. When starches and sugar are combined, weight gain will occur drastically. It is important to note that your new weight has not yet become stable. In other words, it will still show extreme fluctuations after an occasional excess eating. Reintroduce healthy oils into your body such as flax seed oil, extra virgin olive oil and coconut oil. Avoid the unhealthy oils such as vegetable oil and shortening. Butter may also be consumed sparingly.

During and after the transition phase you should not gain any weight. If you gain more than 2 lbs from your LDW (Last Day Weight, the last day you gave yourself an HCG injection, do a Steak Day/ Correction Day.

Breakfast   **Calories**

_____   _____

_____   _____

_____   _____

_____   _____

Lunch

_____   _____

_____   _____

_____   _____

_____   _____

_____   _____

Dinner

_____   _____

_____   _____

_____   _____

_____   _____

_____   _____

_____   _____

Snacks

_____   _____

_____   _____

Total Water Intake: _____   **Total Calories:** _____

Notes / Thoughts: _____

_____

_____

_____

_____

_____

_____

_____

_____

_____

Day 31 : _____ / _____ / _____

Keep Eating Healthy!

Aim for 750 calories

Morning Weight: _____

This transition phase is _every bit as important as the weight loss phase_. The purpose of the transition phase is to maintain metabolic function and customize your metabolic balance with your new weight.

Gradually increase your caloric intake to 1500 calories from 3 meals and snacks. It is important that these meals are comprised of healthy foods and spread out throughout the day. You may now consume any meats, eggs, fruits, cheeses, milk, vegetables and low sugar dairy products. Avoid foods with significant starches such as corn and potatoes. Stay away from sugar completely. When starches and sugar are combined, weight gain will occur drastically. It is important to note that your new weight has not yet become stable. In other words, it will still show extreme fluctuations after an occasional excess eating. Reintroduce healthy oils into your body such as flax seed oil, extra virgin olive oil and coconut oil. Avoid the unhealthy oils such as vegetable oil and shortening. Butter may also be consumed sparingly.

During and after the transition phase you should not gain any weight. If you gain more than 2 lbs from your LDW (Last Day Weight, the last day you gave yourself an HCG injection, do a Steak Day/ Correction Day.

Breakfast   **Calories**

_____   _____

_____   _____

_____   _____

_____   _____

Lunch

_____   _____

_____   _____

_____ _____
_____ _____
_____ _____

Dinner

_____ _____
_____ _____
_____ _____
_____ _____
_____ _____
_____ _____

Snacks

_____ _____
_____ _____

Total Water Intake: _____   **Total Calories:** _____

Notes / Thoughts: _____
_____
_____
_____
_____
_____
_____
_____
_____
_____

Day 32 : _____ / _____ / _____

Keep Eating Healthy!

Aim for 800 calories

Morning Weight: _____

This transition phase is *every bit as important as the weight loss phase*. The purpose of the transition phase is to maintain metabolic function and customize your metabolic balance with your new weight.

Gradually increase your caloric intake to 1500 calories from 3 meals and snacks. It is important that these meals are comprised of healthy foods and spread out throughout the day. You may now consume any meats, eggs, fruits, cheeses, milk, vegetables and low sugar dairy products. Avoid foods with significant starches such as corn and potatoes. Stay away from sugar completely. When starches and sugar are combined, weight gain will occur drastically. It is important to note that your new weight has not yet become stable. In other words, it will still show extreme fluctuations after an occasional excess eating. Reintroduce healthy oils into your body such as flax seed oil, extra virgin olive oil and coconut oil. Avoid the unhealthy oils such as vegetable oil and shortening. Butter may also be consumed sparingly.

During and after the transition phase you should not gain any weight. If you gain more than 2 lbs from your LDW (Last Day Weight, the last day you gave yourself an HCG injection, do a Steak Day/ Correction Day.

Breakfast   **Calories**

_____   _____

_____   _____

_____   _____

_____   _____

Lunch

_____   _____

_____   _____

_____ _____

_____ _____

_____ _____

Dinner

_____ _____

_____ _____

_____ _____

_____ _____

_____ _____

_____ _____

Snacks

_____ _____

_____ _____

Total Water Intake: _____ **Total Calories:** _____

Notes / Thoughts: _____

_____

_____

_____

_____

_____

_____

_____

_____

_____

_____

Day 33 : _____ / _____ / _____

Keep Eating Healthy!

Aim for 850 calories

Morning Weight: _____

This transition phase is _every bit as important as the weight loss phase_.
The purpose of the transition phase is to maintain metabolic function and
customize your metabolic balance with your new weight.

Gradually increase your caloric intake to 1500 calories from 3 meals and
snacks. It is important that these meals are comprised of healthy foods and
spread out throughout the day. You may now consume any meats, eggs,
fruits, cheeses, milk, vegetables and low sugar dairy products. Avoid foods
with significant starches such as corn and potatoes. Stay away from sugar
completely. When starches and sugar are combined, weight gain will occur
drastically. It is important to note that your new weight has not yet become
stable. In other words, it will still show extreme fluctuations after an
occasional excess eating. Reintroduce healthy oils into your body such as
flax seed oil, extra virgin olive oil and coconut oil. Avoid the unhealthy oils
such as vegetable oil and shortening. Butter may also be consumed
sparingly.

During and after the transition phase you should not gain any weight. If
you gain more than 2 lbs from your LDW (Last Day Weight, the last day
you gave yourself an HCG injection, do a Steak Day/ Correction Day.

Breakfast   **Calories**

_____   _____

_____   _____

_____   _____

_____   _____

Lunch

_____   _____

_____   _____

_____ _____

_____ _____

_____ _____

Dinner

_____ _____

_____ _____

_____ _____

_____ _____

_____ _____

_____ _____

Snacks

_____ _____

_____ _____

Total Water Intake: _____   **Total Calories:** _____

Notes / Thoughts: _____

_____

_____

_____

_____

_____

_____

_____

_____

_____

Day 34 : _____ / _____ / _____

Keep Eating Healthy!

Aim for 900 calories

Morning Weight: _____

This transition phase is _every bit as important as the weight loss phase_. The purpose of the transition phase is to maintain metabolic function and customize your metabolic balance with your new weight.

Gradually increase your caloric intake to 1500 calories from 3 meals and snacks. It is important that these meals are comprised of healthy foods and spread out throughout the day. You may now consume any meats, eggs, fruits, cheeses, milk, vegetables and low sugar dairy products. Avoid foods with significant starches such as corn and potatoes. Stay away from sugar completely. When starches and sugar are combined, weight gain will occur drastically. It is important to note that your new weight has not yet become stable. In other words, it will still show extreme fluctuations after an occasional excess eating. Reintroduce healthy oils into your body such as flax seed oil, extra virgin olive oil and coconut oil. Avoid the unhealthy oils such as vegetable oil and shortening. Butter may also be consumed sparingly.

During and after the transition phase you should not gain any weight. If you gain more than 2 lbs from your LDW (Last Day Weight, the last day you gave yourself an HCG injection, do a Steak Day/ Correction Day.

Breakfast   **Calories**

_____   _____

_____   _____

_____   _____

_____   _____

Lunch

_____   _____

_____   _____

_____ _____

_____ _____

_____ _____

Dinner

_____ _____

_____ _____

_____ _____

_____ _____

_____ _____

_____ _____

Snacks

_____ _____

_____ _____

Total Water Intake: _____   **Total Calories:** _____

Notes / Thoughts: _____

_____

_____

_____

_____

_____

_____

_____

_____

_____

Day 35 : _____ / _____ / _____

Keep Eating Healthy!

Aim for 950 calories

Morning Weight: _____

This transition phase is _every bit as important as the weight loss phase_. The purpose of the transition phase is to maintain metabolic function and customize your metabolic balance with your new weight.

Gradually increase your caloric intake to 1500 calories from 3 meals and snacks. It is important that these meals are comprised of healthy foods and spread out throughout the day. You may now consume any meats, eggs, fruits, cheeses, milk, vegetables and low sugar dairy products. Avoid foods with significant starches such as corn and potatoes. Stay away from sugar completely. When starches and sugar are combined, weight gain will occur drastically. It is important to note that your new weight has not yet become stable. In other words, it will still show extreme fluctuations after an occasional excess eating. Reintroduce healthy oils into your body such as flax seed oil, extra virgin olive oil and coconut oil. Avoid the unhealthy oils such as vegetable oil and shortening. Butter may also be consumed sparingly.

During and after the transition phase you should not gain any weight. If you gain more than 2 lbs from your LDW (Last Day Weight, the last day you gave yourself an HCG injection, do a Steak Day/ Correction Day.

Breakfast   **Calories**

_____   _____

_____   _____

_____   _____

_____   _____

Lunch

_____   _____

_____   _____

_____   _____

_____   _____

_____   _____

Dinner

_____   _____

_____   _____

_____   _____

_____   _____

_____   _____

_____   _____

Snacks

_____   _____

_____   _____

Total Water Intake: _____   **Total Calories:** _____

Notes / Thoughts: _____

_____

_____

_____

_____

_____

_____

_____

_____

_____

Day 36 : _____ / _____ / _____

Keep Eating Healthy!

Aim for 1000 calories

Morning Weight: _____

This transition phase is _every bit as important as the weight loss phase_. The purpose of the transition phase is to maintain metabolic function and customize your metabolic balance with your new weight.

Gradually increase your caloric intake to 1500 calories from 3 meals and snacks. It is important that these meals are comprised of healthy foods and spread out throughout the day. You may now consume any meats, eggs, fruits, cheeses, milk, vegetables and low sugar dairy products. Avoid foods with significant starches such as corn and potatoes. Stay away from sugar completely. When starches and sugar are combined, weight gain will occur drastically. It is important to note that your new weight has not yet become stable. In other words, it will still show extreme fluctuations after an occasional excess eating. Reintroduce healthy oils into your body such as flax seed oil, extra virgin olive oil and coconut oil. Avoid the unhealthy oils such as vegetable oil and shortening. Butter may also be consumed sparingly.

During and after the transition phase you should not gain any weight. If you gain more than 2 lbs from your LDW (Last Day Weight, the last day you gave yourself an HCG injection, do a Steak Day/ Correction Day.

Breakfast	Calories

Lunch	

_____   _____

_____   _____

_____   _____

Dinner

_____   _____

_____   _____

_____   _____

_____   _____

_____   _____

Snacks

_____   _____

_____   _____

Total Water Intake: _____   **Total Calories:** _____

Notes / Thoughts: _____

_____

_____

_____

_____

_____

_____

_____

_____

Day 37 : _____ / _____ / _____

Keep Eating Healthy!
Aim for 1050 calories

Morning Weight: _____

This transition phase is _every bit as important as the weight loss phase_. The purpose of the transition phase is to maintain metabolic function and customize your metabolic balance with your new weight.

Gradually increase your caloric intake to 1500 calories from 3 meals and snacks. It is important that these meals are comprised of healthy foods and spread out throughout the day. You may now consume any meats, eggs, fruits, cheeses, milk, vegetables and low sugar dairy products. Avoid foods with significant starches such as corn and potatoes. Stay away from sugar completely. When starches and sugar are combined, weight gain will occur drastically. It is important to note that your new weight has not yet become stable. In other words, it will still show extreme fluctuations after an occasional excess eating. Reintroduce healthy oils into your body such as flax seed oil, extra virgin olive oil and coconut oil. Avoid the unhealthy oils such as vegetable oil and shortening. Butter may also be consumed sparingly.

During and after the transition phase you should not gain any weight. If you gain more than 2 lbs from your LDW (Last Day Weight, the last day you gave yourself an HCG injection, do a Steak Day/ Correction Day.

Breakfast   **Calories**

_____   _____

_____   _____

_____   _____

_____   _____

Lunch

_____   _____

_____   _____

_____ _____

_____ _____

_____ _____

Dinner

_____ _____

_____ _____

_____ _____

_____ _____

_____ _____

_____ _____

Snacks

_____ _____

_____ _____

Total Water Intake: _____   **Total Calories:** _____

Notes / Thoughts: _____

_____

_____

_____

_____

_____

_____

_____

_____

_____

Day 38 : _____ / _____ / _____

Keep Eating Healthy!

Aim for 1100 calories

Morning Weight: _____

This transition phase is _every bit as important as the weight loss phase_. The purpose of the transition phase is to maintain metabolic function and customize your metabolic balance with your new weight.

Gradually increase your caloric intake to 1500 calories from 3 meals and snacks. It is important that these meals are comprised of healthy foods and spread out throughout the day. You may now consume any meats, eggs, fruits, cheeses, milk, vegetables and low sugar dairy products. Avoid foods with significant starches such as corn and potatoes. Stay away from sugar completely. When starches and sugar are combined, weight gain will occur drastically. It is important to note that your new weight has not yet become stable. In other words, it will still show extreme fluctuations after an occasional excess eating. Reintroduce healthy oils into your body such as flax seed oil, extra virgin olive oil and coconut oil. Avoid the unhealthy oils such as vegetable oil and shortening. Butter may also be consumed sparingly.

During and after the transition phase you should not gain any weight. If you gain more than 2 lbs from your LDW (Last Day Weight, the last day you gave yourself an HCG injection, do a Steak Day/ Correction Day.

Breakfast   **Calories**

_____   _____

_____   _____

_____   _____

_____   _____

Lunch

_____   _____

_____   _____

_____   _____

_____   _____

_____   _____

Dinner

_____   _____

_____   _____

_____   _____

_____   _____

_____   _____

Snacks

_____   _____

_____   _____

Total Water Intake: _____   **Total Calories:** _____

Notes / Thoughts: _____

_____

_____

_____

_____

_____

_____

_____

_____

_____

Day 39 : _____ / _____ / _____

Keep Eating Healthy!

Aim for 1150 calories

Morning Weight: _____

This transition phase is _every bit as important as the weight loss phase_. The purpose of the transition phase is to maintain metabolic function and customize your metabolic balance with your new weight.

Gradually increase your caloric intake to 1500 calories from 3 meals and snacks. It is important that these meals are comprised of healthy foods and spread out throughout the day. You may now consume any meats, eggs, fruits, cheeses, milk, vegetables and low sugar dairy products. Avoid foods with significant starches such as corn and potatoes. Stay away from sugar completely. When starches and sugar are combined, weight gain will occur drastically. It is important to note that your new weight has not yet become stable. In other words, it will still show extreme fluctuations after an occasional excess eating. Reintroduce healthy oils into your body such as flax seed oil, extra virgin olive oil and coconut oil. Avoid the unhealthy oils such as vegetable oil and shortening. Butter may also be consumed sparingly.

During and after the transition phase you should not gain any weight. If you gain more than 2 lbs from your LDW (Last Day Weight, the last day you gave yourself an HCG injection, do a Steak Day/ Correction Day.

Breakfast   **Calories**

_____   _____

_____   _____

_____   _____

_____   _____

Lunch

_____   _____

_____   _____

_____   _____

_____   _____

_____   _____

Dinner

_____   _____

_____   _____

_____   _____

_____   _____

_____   _____

_____   _____

Snacks

_____   _____

_____   _____

Total Water Intake: _____   **Total Calories:** _____

Notes / Thoughts: _____

_____

_____

_____

_____

_____

_____

_____

_____

_____

Day 40 : _____ / _____ / _____

Keep Eating Healthy!

Aim for 1200 calories

Morning Weight: _____

This transition phase is _every bit as important as the weight loss phase_. The purpose of the transition phase is to maintain metabolic function and customize your metabolic balance with your new weight.

Gradually increase your caloric intake to 1500 calories from 3 meals and snacks. It is important that these meals are comprised of healthy foods and spread out throughout the day. You may now consume any meats, eggs, fruits, cheeses, milk, vegetables and low sugar dairy products. Avoid foods with significant starches such as corn and potatoes. Stay away from sugar completely. When starches and sugar are combined, weight gain will occur drastically. It is important to note that your new weight has not yet become stable. In other words, it will still show extreme fluctuations after an occasional excess eating. Reintroduce healthy oils into your body such as flax seed oil, extra virgin olive oil and coconut oil. Avoid the unhealthy oils such as vegetable oil and shortening. Butter may also be consumed sparingly.

During and after the transition phase you should not gain any weight. If you gain more than 2 lbs from your LDW (Last Day Weight, the last day you gave yourself an HCG injection, do a Steak Day/ Correction Day.

Breakfast   **Calories**

_____   _____

_____   _____

_____   _____

_____   _____

Lunch

_____   _____

_____   _____

_____ _____

_____ _____

_____ _____

Dinner

_____ _____

_____ _____

_____ _____

_____ _____

_____ _____

_____ _____

Snacks

_____ _____

_____ _____

Total Water Intake: _____   **Total Calories:** _____

Notes / Thoughts: _____

_____

_____

_____

_____

_____

_____

_____

_____

_____

Day 41 : _____ / _____ / _____

Keep Eating Healthy!

Aim for 1250 calories

Morning Weight: _____

This transition phase is _every bit as important as the weight loss phase_. The purpose of the transition phase is to maintain metabolic function and customize your metabolic balance with your new weight.

Gradually increase your caloric intake to 1500 calories from 3 meals and snacks. It is important that these meals are comprised of healthy foods and spread out throughout the day. You may now consume any meats, eggs, fruits, cheeses, milk, vegetables and low sugar dairy products. Avoid foods with significant starches such as corn and potatoes. Stay away from sugar completely. When starches and sugar are combined, weight gain will occur drastically. It is important to note that your new weight has not yet become stable. In other words, it will still show extreme fluctuations after an occasional excess eating. Reintroduce healthy oils into your body such as flax seed oil, extra virgin olive oil and coconut oil. Avoid the unhealthy oils such as vegetable oil and shortening. Butter may also be consumed sparingly.

During and after the transition phase you should not gain any weight. If you gain more than 2 lbs from your LDW (Last Day Weight, the last day you gave yourself an HCG injection, do a Steak Day/ Correction Day.

Breakfast   **Calories**

_____   _____

_____   _____

_____   _____

_____   _____

Lunch

_____   _____

_____   _____

_____   _____

_____   _____

_____   _____

Dinner

_____   _____

_____   _____

_____   _____

_____   _____

_____   _____

_____   _____

Snacks

_____   _____

_____   _____

Total Water Intake: _____   **Total Calories:** _____

Notes / Thoughts: _____

_____

_____

_____

_____

_____

_____

_____

_____

_____

Day 42 : _____ / _____ / _____

Keep Eating Healthy!

Aim for 1300 calories

Morning Weight: _____

This transition phase is _every bit as important as the weight loss phase_. The purpose of the transition phase is to maintain metabolic function and customize your metabolic balance with your new weight.

Gradually increase your caloric intake to 1500 calories from 3 meals and snacks. It is important that these meals are comprised of healthy foods and spread out throughout the day. You may now consume any meats, eggs, fruits, cheeses, milk, vegetables and low sugar dairy products. Avoid foods with significant starches such as corn and potatoes. Stay away from sugar completely. When starches and sugar are combined, weight gain will occur drastically. It is important to note that your new weight has not yet become stable. In other words, it will still show extreme fluctuations after an occasional excess eating. Reintroduce healthy oils into your body such as flax seed oil, extra virgin olive oil and coconut oil. Avoid the unhealthy oils such as vegetable oil and shortening. Butter may also be consumed sparingly.

During and after the transition phase you should not gain any weight. If you gain more than 2 lbs from your LDW (Last Day Weight, the last day you gave yourself an HCG injection, do a Steak Day/ Correction Day.

Breakfast   **Calories**

_____   _____

_____   _____

_____   _____

_____   _____

Lunch

_____   _____

_____   _____

_____   _____

_____   _____

_____   _____

Dinner

_____   _____

_____   _____

_____   _____

_____   _____

_____   _____

_____   _____

Snacks

_____   _____

_____   _____

Total Water Intake: _____   **Total Calories:** _____

Notes / Thoughts: _____

_____

_____

_____

_____

_____

_____

_____

_____

_____

Day 43 : _____ / _____ / _____

Keep Eating Healthy!

Aim for 1350 calories

Morning Weight: _____

This transition phase is _every bit as important as the weight loss phase_. The purpose of the transition phase is to maintain metabolic function and customize your metabolic balance with your new weight.

Gradually increase your caloric intake to 1500 calories from 3 meals and snacks. It is important that these meals are comprised of healthy foods and spread out throughout the day. You may now consume any meats, eggs, fruits, cheeses, milk, vegetables and low sugar dairy products. Avoid foods with significant starches such as corn and potatoes. Stay away from sugar completely. When starches and sugar are combined, weight gain will occur drastically. It is important to note that your new weight has not yet become stable. In other words, it will still show extreme fluctuations after an occasional excess eating. Reintroduce healthy oils into your body such as flax seed oil, extra virgin olive oil and coconut oil. Avoid the unhealthy oils such as vegetable oil and shortening. Butter may also be consumed sparingly.

During and after the transition phase you should not gain any weight. If you gain more than 2 lbs from your LDW (Last Day Weight, the last day you gave yourself an HCG injection, do a Steak Day/ Correction Day.

Breakfast   **Calories**

_____   _____

_____   _____

_____   _____

_____   _____

Lunch

_____   _____

_____   _____

_____ _____

_____ _____

_____ _____

Dinner

_____ _____

_____ _____

_____ _____

_____ _____

_____ _____

_____ _____

Snacks

_____ _____

_____ _____

Total Water Intake: _____   **Total Calories:** _____

Notes / Thoughts: _____

_____

_____

_____

_____

_____

_____

_____

_____

_____

_____

Day 44 : _____ / _____ / _____

Keep Eating Healthy!

Aim for 1400 calories

Morning Weight: _____

This transition phase is _every bit as important as the weight loss phase_. The purpose of the transition phase is to maintain metabolic function and customize your metabolic balance with your new weight.

Gradually increase your caloric intake to 1500 calories from 3 meals and snacks. It is important that these meals are comprised of healthy foods and spread out throughout the day. You may now consume any meats, eggs, fruits, cheeses, milk, vegetables and low sugar dairy products. Avoid foods with significant starches such as corn and potatoes. Stay away from sugar completely. When starches and sugar are combined, weight gain will occur drastically. It is important to note that your new weight has not yet become stable. In other words, it will still show extreme fluctuations after an occasional excess eating. Reintroduce healthy oils into your body such as flax seed oil, extra virgin olive oil and coconut oil. Avoid the unhealthy oils such as vegetable oil and shortening. Butter may also be consumed sparingly.

During and after the transition phase you should not gain any weight. If you gain more than 2 lbs from your LDW (Last Day Weight, the last day you gave yourself an HCG injection, do a Steak Day/ Correction Day.

Breakfast   **Calories**

_____   _____

_____   _____

_____   _____

_____   _____

Lunch

_____   _____

_____   _____

_____ _____

_____ _____

_____ _____

Dinner

_____ _____

_____ _____

_____ _____

_____ _____

_____ _____

_____ _____

Snacks

_____ _____

_____ _____

Total Water Intake: _____   **Total Calories:** _____

Notes / Thoughts: _____

_____

_____

_____

_____

_____

_____

_____

_____

_____

Day 45 : _____ / _____ / _____

Keep Eating Healthy!

Aim for 1450 calories

Morning Weight: _____

This transition phase is _every bit as important as the weight loss phase_. The purpose of the transition phase is to maintain metabolic function and customize your metabolic balance with your new weight.

Gradually increase your caloric intake to 1500 calories from 3 meals and snacks. It is important that these meals are comprised of healthy foods and spread out throughout the day. You may now consume any meats, eggs, fruits, cheeses, milk, vegetables and low sugar dairy products. Avoid foods with significant starches such as corn and potatoes. Stay away from sugar completely. When starches and sugar are combined, weight gain will occur drastically. It is important to note that your new weight has not yet become stable. In other words, it will still show extreme fluctuations after an occasional excess eating. Reintroduce healthy oils into your body such as flax seed oil, extra virgin olive oil and coconut oil. Avoid the unhealthy oils such as vegetable oil and shortening. Butter may also be consumed sparingly.

During and after the transition phase you should not gain any weight. If you gain more than 2 lbs from your LDW (Last Day Weight, the last day you gave yourself an HCG injection, do a Steak Day/ Correction Day.

Breakfast   **Calories**

_____   _____

_____   _____

_____   _____

_____   _____

Lunch

_____   _____

_____   _____

_____   _____
_____   _____
_____   _____

Dinner

_____   _____
_____   _____
_____   _____
_____   _____
_____   _____

Snacks

_____   _____
_____   _____

Total Water Intake: _____   **Total Calories:** _____

Notes / Thoughts: _____
_____
_____
_____
_____
_____
_____
_____
_____
_____

Day 46 : _____ / _____ / _____

Keep Eating Healthy!

Aim for 1500 calories

Morning Weight: _____

This transition phase is _every bit as important as the weight loss phase_. The purpose of the transition phase is to maintain metabolic function and customize your metabolic balance with your new weight.

Gradually increase your caloric intake to 1500 calories from 3 meals and snacks. It is important that these meals are comprised of healthy foods and spread out throughout the day. You may now consume any meats, eggs, fruits, cheeses, milk, vegetables and low sugar dairy products. Avoid foods with significant starches such as corn and potatoes. Stay away from sugar completely. When starches and sugar are combined, weight gain will occur drastically. It is important to note that your new weight has not yet become stable. In other words, it will still show extreme fluctuations after an occasional excess eating. Reintroduce healthy oils into your body such as flax seed oil, extra virgin olive oil and coconut oil. Avoid the unhealthy oils such as vegetable oil and shortening. Butter may also be consumed sparingly.

During and after the transition phase you should not gain any weight. If you gain more than 2 lbs from your LDW (Last Day Weight, the last day you gave yourself an HCG injection, do a Steak Day/ Correction Day.

Breakfast   **Calories**

_____   _____

_____   _____

_____   _____

_____   _____

Lunch

_____   _____

_____   _____

_____ _____

_____ _____

_____ _____

Dinner

_____ _____

_____ _____

_____ _____

_____ _____

_____ _____

Snacks

_____ _____

_____ _____

Total Water Intake: _____   **Total Calories:** _____

Notes / Thoughts: _____

_____

_____

_____

_____

_____

_____

_____

_____

_____

Day 47 : _____ / _____ / _____

Keep Eating Healthy!
Aim for 1500 calories

Morning Weight: _____

This transition phase is _every bit as important as the weight loss phase_.
The purpose of the transition phase is to maintain metabolic function and
customize your metabolic balance with your new weight.

Gradually increase your caloric intake to 1500 calories from 3 meals and
snacks. It is important that these meals are comprised of healthy foods and
spread out throughout the day. You may now consume any meats, eggs,
fruits, cheeses, milk, vegetables and low sugar dairy products. Avoid foods
with significant starches such as corn and potatoes. Stay away from sugar
completely. When starches and sugar are combined, weight gain will occur
drastically. It is important to note that your new weight has not yet become
stable. In other words, it will still show extreme fluctuations after an
occasional excess eating. Reintroduce healthy oils into your body such as
flax seed oil, extra virgin olive oil and coconut oil. Avoid the unhealthy oils
such as vegetable oil and shortening. Butter may also be consumed
sparingly.

During and after the transition phase you should not gain any weight. If
you gain more than 2 lbs from your LDW (Last Day Weight, the last day
you gave yourself an HCG injection, do a Steak Day/ Correction Day.

Breakfast   **Calories**

_____   _____

_____   _____

_____   _____

_____   _____

Lunch

_____   _____

_____   _____

_____ _____

_____ _____

_____ _____

Dinner

_____ _____

_____ _____

_____ _____

_____ _____

_____ _____

_____ _____

Snacks

_____ _____

_____ _____

Total Water Intake: _____   **Total Calories:** _____

Notes / Thoughts: _____

_____

_____

_____

_____

_____

_____

_____

_____

_____

CONGRATULATIONS!

You have made it to Phase 4 – Your new healthy lifestyle!

This is the lifetime maintenance phase of the program. Continue to keep sugars to a minimum, introduce starches back to your diet *very slowly* and consume sugars, starches and healthy carbs in moderation. We recommend whole grains, oats, wheat bread, etc… Avoid heavy starch and sugars such as those found in potatoes, yams and rice. Hydrogenated oils typically found in some canned goods and pastries should be avoided.

Strive to stay away from processed foods. Avoid high volumes of fructose syrup in such things as canned fruit, fruit drinks and soda.

Continue to eat proteins and stay away from heavily processed or fast foods.

If you did not reach your weight loss goal during the 1st Cycle, you can now continue onto Cycle 2. This Cycle is a repeat of the 1st Cycle. The time off needed between each cycle will vary but is usually 2-4 weeks. After this break, you can continue until you reach your intended goal. Many individuals have lost in excess of 150 lbs over several courses of the diet.

A few additional pages have been included in this tracker to allow you to, if you desire, continue to log your daily calories to help you transition into your new healthy lifestyle!

Date: _____   **Morning Weight:** _____

Breakfast   **Calories**

_____   _____

_____   _____

_____   _____

_____   _____

Lunch

_____   _____

_____   _____

_____   _____

_____   _____

_____   _____

Dinner

_____   _____

_____   _____

_____   _____

_____   _____

_____   _____

_____   _____

Snacks

_____   _____

_____   _____

Total Water Intake: _____   **Total Calories:** _____

Date: _____   **Morning Weight:** _____

Breakfast   **Calories**

_____   _____

_____   _____

_____   _____

_____   _____

Lunch

_____   _____

_____   _____

_____   _____

_____   _____

_____   _____

Dinner

_____   _____

_____   _____

_____   _____

_____   _____

_____   _____

Snacks

_____   _____

_____   _____

Total Water Intake: _____   **Total Calories:** _____

Date: _____   **Morning Weight:** _____

Breakfast   **Calories**

_____   _____
_____   _____
_____   _____
_____   _____

Lunch

_____   _____
_____   _____
_____   _____
_____   _____

Dinner

_____   _____
_____   _____
_____   _____
_____   _____
_____   _____

Snacks

_____   _____
_____   _____

Total Water Intake: _____   **Total Calories:** _____

Date: _____ **Morning Weight:** _____

Breakfast   **Calories**

_____   _____

_____   _____

_____   _____

_____   _____

Lunch

_____   _____

_____   _____

_____   _____

_____   _____

_____   _____

Dinner

_____   _____

_____   _____

_____   _____

_____   _____

_____   _____

Snacks

_____   _____

_____   _____

Total Water Intake: _____   **Total Calories:** _____

Date: _____   Morning Weight: _____

Breakfast   **Calories**

_____   _____

_____   _____

_____   _____

_____   _____

Lunch

_____   _____

_____   _____

_____   _____

_____   _____

_____   _____

Dinner

_____   _____

_____   _____

_____   _____

_____   _____

_____   _____

Snacks

_____   _____

_____   _____

Total Water Intake: _____   **Total Calories:** _____

Date: _____ **Morning Weight:** _____

Breakfast   **Calories**

_____   _____

_____   _____

_____   _____

_____   _____

Lunch

_____   _____

_____   _____

_____   _____

_____   _____

_____   _____

Dinner

_____   _____

_____   _____

_____   _____

_____   _____

_____   _____

_____   _____

Snacks

_____   _____

_____   _____

Total Water Intake: _____   **Total Calories:** _____

Date: _____   Morning Weight: _____

Breakfast   **Calories**

_____   _____

_____   _____

_____   _____

_____   _____

Lunch

_____   _____

_____   _____

_____   _____

_____   _____

_____   _____

Dinner

_____   _____

_____   _____

_____   _____

_____   _____

_____   _____

_____   _____

Snacks

_____   _____

_____   _____

Total Water Intake: _____   **Total Calories:** _____

Date: _____ **Morning Weight:** _____

Breakfast   **Calories**

_____   _____

_____   _____

_____   _____

_____   _____

Lunch

_____   _____

_____   _____

_____   _____

_____   _____

Dinner

_____   _____

_____   _____

_____   _____

_____   _____

_____   _____

Snacks

_____   _____

_____   _____

Total Water Intake: _____   **Total Calories:** _____

Date: _____   **Morning Weight:** _____

Breakfast   **Calories**

_____   _____

_____   _____

_____   _____

Lunch

_____   _____

_____   _____

_____   _____

_____   _____

Dinner

_____   _____

_____   _____

_____   _____

_____   _____

Snacks

_____   _____

_____   _____

Total Water Intake: _____   **Total Calories:** _____

Date: _____   **Morning Weight:** _____

Breakfast   **Calories**

_____   _____

_____   _____

_____   _____

_____   _____

Lunch

_____   _____

_____   _____

_____   _____

_____   _____

_____   _____

Dinner

_____   _____

_____   _____

_____   _____

_____   _____

_____   _____

_____   _____

Snacks

_____   _____

_____   _____

Total Water Intake: _____   **Total Calories:** _____

Date: _____ **Morning Weight:** _____

Breakfast   **Calories**

_____   _____

_____   _____

_____   _____

_____   _____

Lunch

_____   _____

_____   _____

_____   _____

_____   _____

_____   _____

Dinner

_____   _____

_____   _____

_____   _____

_____   _____

_____   _____

Snacks

_____   _____

_____   _____

Total Water Intake: _____   **Total Calories:** _____

Date: _____ **Morning Weight:** _____

Breakfast   **Calories**

_____   _____

_____   _____

_____   _____

_____

Lunch

_____   _____

_____   _____

_____   _____

_____   _____

_____

Dinner

_____   _____

_____   _____

_____   _____

_____   _____

_____   _____

_____

Snacks

_____   _____

_____   _____

Total Water Intake: _____   **Total Calories:** _____

Date: _____   Morning Weight: _____

Breakfast   **Calories**

_____   _____

_____   _____

_____   _____

_____   _____

Lunch

_____   _____

_____   _____

_____   _____

_____   _____

Dinner

_____   _____

_____   _____

_____   _____

_____   _____

_____   _____

Snacks

_____   _____

_____   _____

Total Water Intake: _____   **Total Calories:** _____

Date: _____   **Morning Weight:** _____

Breakfast   **Calories**

_____   _____

_____   _____

_____   _____

_____   _____

Lunch

_____   _____

_____   _____

_____   _____

_____   _____

Dinner

_____   _____

_____   _____

_____   _____

_____   _____

_____   _____

Snacks

_____   _____

_____   _____

Total Water Intake: _____   **Total Calories:** _____

Date: _____   **Morning Weight:** _____

Breakfast

                                        Calories

_____ _____

_____ _____

_____ _____

_____ _____

Lunch

_____ _____

_____ _____

_____ _____

_____ _____

_____ _____

Dinner

_____ _____

_____ _____

_____ _____

_____ _____

_____ _____

_____ _____

Snacks

_____ _____

_____ _____

Total Water Intake: _____   **Total Calories:** _____

Date: _____ **Morning Weight:** _____

Breakfast   **Calories**

_____   _____

_____   _____

_____   _____

_____   _____

Lunch

_____   _____

_____   _____

_____   _____

_____   _____

_____   _____

Dinner

_____   _____

_____   _____

_____   _____

_____   _____

_____   _____

_____   _____

Snacks

_____   _____

_____   _____

Total Water Intake: _____   **Total Calories:** _____

Calorie Counts for HCG Foods

Fruits

Apple	100 calories
Strawberries	1 cup = 46 calories
Orange	70 calories
1/2 Grapefruit	60 calories

Vegetables

You may have a vegetable serving sized to your preference. However, you must count your calories accordingly.

Spinach	1 cup = 7 calories
Tomato, cherry	One = 3 calories
Tomato, medium	One = 22 calories
Celery, medium 8" stalk	One = 8 calories
Beet greens	1 cup = 8 calories
Chard	1 cup = 7 calories
Chicory	1 cup = 7 calories
Lettuce	1 cup = 5 calories
Onion, medium 1/8" slice	One slice = 6 calories
Onion, chopped	One TBSP = 4 calories
Red Radish	One = 1 calorie
Cucumber, sliced	One slice = 6 calorie
Cucumber, chopped	1 cup = 16 calories
Asparagus	7" spear = 3 calories
Cabbage, shredded	1 cup = 18 calories

Proteins: 3.5 oz. of all Meats

Chicken Breast	114 calories
Ground Beef, 95%	137 calories
Sirloin	131 calories
Beef Tenderloin	153 calories
Ground Veal	144 calories
Veal, Scaloppini	112 calories
Crab, Alaskan King	84 calories
Lobster	90 calories
Tilapia	96 calories
Halibut	110 calories
Orange Roughy	76 calories
Cod	82 calories
Red Snapper	100 calories
Grouper	92 calories
Sword Fish	121 calories
Pollock	92 calories
Shrimp	106 calories

Starch

Melba toast, one piece	20 calories
Alessie Breadstick, one	20 calories

Made in the USA
Columbia, SC
12 September 2022